STEVEN SPIELBERG

Crazy for Movies

SUSAN GOLDMAN RUBIN

Harry N. Abrams, Inc., New York

To Michael, my companion at the movies

Acknowledgments:

Many people helped me with this book. First of all, I want to thank members of Steven Spielberg's family—his mother, Leah Adler; his father, Arnold Spielberg; and his sisters Anne, Sue, and Nancy. I greatly appreciate their warmth in sharing reminiscences, and their trust in lending me precious family photos. I thank Richard Dreyfuss, Jerry Molen, Ariana Richards, and John Williams for graciously granting me interviews. And a special thank you to Allen Daviau for giving me so much of his time. I am grateful to Daisy Miller and Janet Keller at the Survivors of the Shoah Visual History Foundation for their generous cooperation. And I especially thank Cindy Chang, Chante Hardesty, and Bette Einbinder at Universal Studios for assisting me with photo research. My thanks also to Bonnie Mansdorf, Rabbi Benjamin Herson, and Daniel Neman. I am particularly grateful to Stephen Fraser, who hatched this idea with me in the first place. Finally, in this list, come my editors Laaren Brown and Howard Reeves. I thank them for their wholehearted support in working on this book. As always, this list would be incomplete without expressing thanks to my agent George M. Nicholson for his guidance as well as encouragement. And of course, a big thank you to my son Andy for all his help. Most of all I thank my husband, Michael, for going to so many movies with me and understanding my enthusiasm.

Designer: Edward Miller

Library of Congress Cataloging-in-Publication Data

Rubin, Susan Goldman
   Steven Spielberg: crazy for movies / by Susan Goldman Rubin
     p. cm.
   Includes bibliographical references and index.
   ISBN 0-8109-4492-8
   1. Spielberg, Steven, 1946- —Juvenile literature. 2. Motion picture producers and
directors—United States—Biography—Juvenile literature. [1. Spielberg, Steven, 1946-
2. Motion picture producers and directors.] I. Title.

   PN1998.3.S65 R83 2001
   791.43'0233'092—dc21
   [B]
   00-069973

Text copyright © 2001 Susan Goldman Rubin
Copyright © 2001 Harry N. Abrams, Inc.
For photo credits, see page 91.
Published in 2001 by Harry N. Abrams, Incorporated, New York
All rights reserved. No part of the contents of this book may be reproduced without the written permission of the publisher.
Printed and bound in Hong Kong
10 9 8 7 6 5 4 3 2 1

Harry N. Abrams, Inc.
100 Fifth Avenue
New York, N.Y. 10011
www.abramsbooks.com

Contents

Firelight   4

Poltergeist   9

The Last Shootout   14

A Boy's Life   20

Amblin'   24

Duel and *The Sugarland Express*   28

Jaws   36

Close Encounters   42

From *Raiders of the Lost Ark* to *E.T.*   46

The Color Purple and *Empire of the Sun*   54

Jurassic Park   60

Schindler's List   67

The Shoah Foundation   75

DreamWorks Presents *Saving Private Ryan*   78

Coming Attractions   86

   References and Resources   88

   Glossary of Filmmaking Terms   90

   Index   92

   Author's Note   94

Firelight

One night when Steven Spielberg was ten, his father woke him up and took him out to the desert near where they lived in Phoenix, Arizona. They spread out a blanket and lay on their backs looking up at the sky. Steven's father, Arnold Spielberg, liked astronomy and hoped to see a comet that was supposed to appear. Instead, they saw a meteor shower. "The stars were just tremendous," recalled Arnold. "They were so intense it was frightening." He gave Steven a scientific explanation of what was happening.

"But I didn't want to hear that," said Steven. "I wanted to think of them as falling stars." That memory of falling stars stayed with him and inspired his first full-length movie, *Firelight*. Steven later said that the meteors showed him a "world beyond the earth," and left him "wanting to tell stories not of this world."

At sixteen Steven started to tell those stories.

His first feature-length movie was a science-fiction thriller called *Firelight*. *Firelight* told a story about mysterious aliens flying to earth to abduct humans for an extraterrestial zoo. Steven wrote the story and directed the film. At that time—the early 1960s—many people claimed to have spotted flying saucers and other UFOs (unidentified flying objects), and these reports fascinated Steven.

He spent nearly his whole junior year of high

Baby Steven with Arnold and Leah, *top*. Steven in school, *left*. Steven (left) and a friend filming in the desert, *opposite page*.

"I was more or less a boy with a passion for a hobby that grew out of control and consumed me."

school producing the film. "I was more or less a boy with a passion for a hobby that grew out of control and consumed me," he said. Steven and his sister Anne belonged to the drama club at Arcadia High School in Phoenix. Steven cast their friends in the different roles and recruited drama students from Arizona State University because to him they looked like grown-ups. He shot the movie on the weekends.

"Everybody wanted to be a part of it," recalls Anne. "The moment he started a project it was like the Pied Piper. Everybody in the neighborhood wanted to have something to do with it. I used to get jealous. The girl who was the most popular girl in *my* class, she'd come over to be in Steve's movie. It was exciting and he made it fun and the kids were totally committed. They worked their butts off."

"My house was a *total* studio," remembers Steven's mother, Leah Adler. "Steve came along and took my house away. And the next thing on the menu was scaffolding, gel lights, a dolly."

Everyone in the Spielberg family helped Steve with *Firelight*. In one scene a maid, played by Anne's friend Tina, was supposed to forget that she was cooking cherries jubilee in the pressure cooker. Leah herself loaded thirty cans of cherry pie filling in her pressure cooker and allowed Steve to blow it up. For months afterward, says Leah, cherries and cherry juice oozed from her kitchen cupboards.

Anne typed the script and was script supervisor. During filming she pushed the dolly, a device for moving the camera. The dolly was actually their mother's serving cart. "Steve sat on it with the camera," Anne recalls, "and I pushed it down the hall so that he could get a zoom shot." Sometimes Anne didn't feel like participating. "Steve would pull me out of my own things to work on his movies," she says. "I didn't want to do

it. Suddenly it became a threat." Steven would say, "If you don't do this you're not in my next movie." And Anne wanted to be part of his projects. "Whatever he was doing looked better than anything I could think of doing," she says.

For *Firelight*, Anne and their nine-year-old sister, Sue, did the visual effects. Steven wanted to show firelight absorbing somebody. "He created a special effect," says Sue. "I was what we called 'the musher.' We took Vaseline and put it between two blue cels or two red cels depending on the firelight that attacked the person." While Sue rubbed the plates together, Steven took the picture through them and it looked like something swirling around. This was "firelight."

Sue also held hot lights and remembers once getting burned. But she didn't mind. "We all got into it with him," she says. "It was a lot of fun. We read the script, we acted in parts. My little sister got 'killed' off."

Nancy, their youngest sister, then about four years old, starred in the movie. She played the little girl snatched by alien firelight. Outdoors, Steve directed Nancy to crawl toward a tree while staring up at the sun. "Reach out and don't squint," he told her.

"Nancy had to crawl toward this blinding light," remembers Leah. "I'm surprised she still has vision."

Steven's father Arnold Spielberg, a computer engineer, not only invested money in the movie, he rigged the lights for indoor filming and designed miniature sets. At the time he was working away from home at IBM in San Jose, California. "I would come home every three weeks and try to help Steven with something, and then go back to work," recalls Arnold. "I was totally amazed at the way it was going. I made any special construction, any electrical stuff he needed. To make *Firelight* he wanted to show a 'situation board,' and it was a map of a town. We had lights lighting up. And I wired all the lights up for him. They would be flashing as the firelight was attacking different places.

"Then he needed another special effect of having trucks going up a mountain. Well, we didn't have a bunch of army trucks. So we bought these little miniature trucks. And we made a papier-mâché mountain.

Anne, Sue, and Nancy, *opposite page*. Steven filming *Firelight, right*.

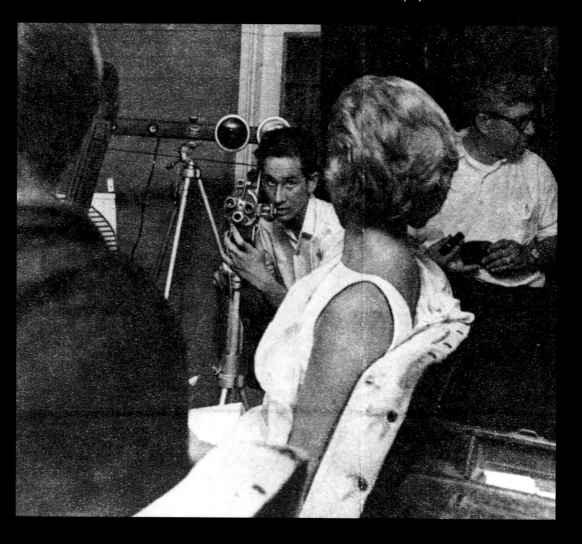

And he had the trucks going up the mountain. He would move them a quarter of an inch . . . and he would take a 'stop motion.' He'd take one shot and move the truck another quarter of an inch. And when it was played back, they were actually going up the mountain!"

Steven did the splicing and editing all by himself. Often he would pretend he was sick so that he could stay home from school and work on his movie. Leah knew he was faking, but she went along with it. Even then she recognized Steven's burning desire to make movies.

To record a soundtrack for *Firelight*—home-movie cameras were silent in those days—he set up a microphone in the living room and recorded the actors speaking their lines as the film was projected on a wall. Then he added sound effects and a musical score. His mother, a classical pianist, helped him. Steven played clarinet in the high school band and in the drama club's orchestra, and shared his mother's love of music.

At last Steven and the entire cast and crew saw the final print of *Firelight* in his living room. When he saw the film, Steven said, "I knew what I wanted. I wanted Hollywood."

The movie premiered on March 24, 1964, at the Phoenix Little Theater. Arnold rented the theater for the night, and Leah climbed up on a ladder to put the title of the film on the marquee. Tickets sold for seventy-five cents a head and earned Steven a profit of one dollar, which he gave to the Perry Institute, a home for mentally handicapped children.

The day after the premiere, Steven and his family left Phoenix and moved to California. But Steven's determination to become a filmmaker remained fixed. Years later, when he became a professional, *Firelight*, the movie inspired by those shooting stars, evolved into *Close Encounters of the Third Kind*. Over and over again Steven turned to the same ideas. His experiences growing up would prove to be a driving force behind his art.

Steven standing on a jeep to film *Firelight, above.*

Poltergeist

"I can always trace a movie idea back to my childhood," Steven once said.

He was born on December 18, 1946, in Cincinnati, Ohio, and spent his first three years in the Jewish neighborhood of Avondale. From the start everyone thought he seemed unusual.

"Different," recalls a next-door neighbor.

"Energetic," remembers his father. "Curious. Wanting to get into everything. Wanting to ask questions about things."

Says his mother, "I didn't know that everybody didn't have kids like him. . . . If I had known better, I would have taken him to a psychiatrist, and there never would have been an *E.T.*" His maternal grandmother, Jennie Posner, who lived nearby, adored him. "My mother saw in Steve something so special," recalls Leah. "'You mark my words,' she would say, 'the world will hear of him.'"

Once, when Steven was about two years old, he was walking past a toy store with Leah and saw a toy Greyhound bus that he wanted. She wouldn't buy it for him. "Steven had such a tantrum," she recalls, "that the rabbi, who was passing by, called my mother, and Grandma bought it for him." At home he played with the bus by balancing it on the very edge of the table with two wheels hanging over the side—he was already trying stunts and special effects.

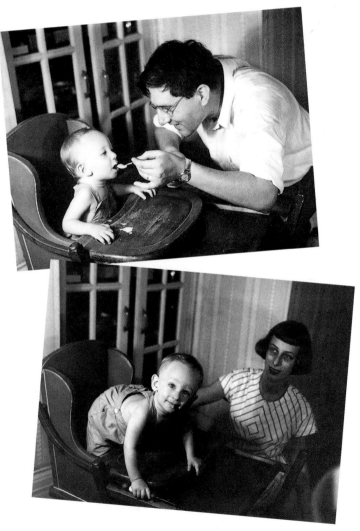

Baby Steven with Arnold, *top,* and with Leah, *bottom.*

Steven, Jennie, and Leah, *top*. Philip and Jennie, *center*. Fievel the mouse, Philip's namesake, from An American Tail, *bottom*.

Steve's grandmother Jennie (he called her Mama) taught English to Holocaust survivors who were preparing for citizenship. One of her pupils had been imprisoned at Auschwitz and had numbers tattooed on his arm. Steven remembered the man showing him the tattoo. "He would roll up his sleeve and say, 'I have a magic trick.'" He pointed to a six. And then he crooked his elbow and said, 'Now it's a nine.'"

Listening to survivors' horror stories about the Nazis stayed with Steven through the years and may have inspired him to make *Schindler's List*. "The Holocaust has been part of my life, just based on what my parents would say at the dinner table," he recalled.

His grandfather Philip Posner (he called him Dadda), an orthodox Jew, loved music and dancing, and he was a gifted storyteller. Steven said, "I remember hearing stories from him when I was four or five, and I'd be breathless, sitting on the edge of his knee." Grandpa Philip's Yiddish name was Fievel. When Steven grew up and made *An American Tail*, an animated movie about a mouse who immigrates to America, he named his hero Fievel after his grandpa.

Steven may have inherited his love of movies from his grandmother Jennie. "She was an avid moviegoer," recalls Leah. "Every Thursday she took a bag of candy and saw three or four movies alone."

Steven didn't see *his* first movie until he moved to New Jersey. The family went there when he was three years old because his father had a new job. Steven has said, "I was afraid of trees, clouds, the wind, the dark." Even a clown doll gave him the creeps. Years later he used all of these terrifying images in his horror movie *Poltergeist*.

The first movie Steven Spielberg ever saw—he was five years old—was *The Greatest Show on Earth,* a potboiler about life behind the scenes at a circus. The movie disappointed him because he thought he would see a real circus. For him the most memorable part of the film was a train wreck near the end. But the next movies he saw, Disney's *Bambi* and *Snow White and the Seven Dwarfs*, really scared him. "I came home screaming from *Snow White* when I was eight years old," said Steven, "and tried to hide under the covers."

Outside Steven's bedroom window was a spindly tree. At night, with the streetlight shining on the tree, the swaying branches cast eerie shadows on the walls of his bedroom. To Steven the tree appeared sinister, says Leah: "a bad, bad tree of evil."

Steven also thought there was a monster under his bed, another in his closet, and ghostly creatures living in a crack above his closet door. Petrified, he would jump out of bed and run to his mother's room. "He appeared at my bedside nightly," she says. "He was always frightened. Things would wake him and startle him."

When his sisters were born—Anne in 1949, Sue in 1953, and Nancy in 1956—he figured out a way to conquer his fears by scaring *them*. "We loved to be scared," says Sue. "Part of it was really fun. He used to tell us terrifying stories."

"He would come in sometimes," says Anne, "and say, 'Want a bedtime story?' I'd go, 'No!' He'd go, 'This is a good one. It's called I'm the Moon.' He gave me a phobia for a couple of years. I had nightmares about the moon."

Steven would stand outside Anne's window and pretend that he was the moon, who had come down to earth. "My bed was right under the window," she says. "Sometimes he would just scratch on the glass. And I would say, 'I know it's you. I'm not opening the curtains.' He would just keep on scratching. I'd say, 'Steve! Stop it! I know it's you.' But I was still scared. So

The Spielberg home in New Jersey (the bad, bad tree of evil is in the back), *top*. Baby Anne with Steven, *center*. Anne, Sue, and Steven, *bottom*.

of course I had to open the curtains to see. And he'd have the flashlight under his chin. Or he had this model plastic skull, a life-sized skull. He would drip candle wax on to make it look as though flesh had dissolved. And he'd have the flashlight under the skull."

The children's games always involved making up stories. "Mom would say, 'How nice, the children are playing,'" says Nancy. "I would run into the room screaming and clawing and hanging on to my mom's leg saying, 'Make him stop! Make him stop! He's playing Tornado!'"

The game Tornado went like this, recalls Nancy. "We were sitting with our dolls and Steven was singing as if he was on the radio. Then he interrupted himself to bring us an important message."

"He'd say, 'We interrupt this program to announce that a tornado is coming to attack Nancy and Sue,'" remembers Sue. "'Hurry! Get to a shelter!' he'd say. Steve was the launching pad. He'd lie down on the floor in the hallway and would flip us over his head to 'safety' in the shelter. Only one of us would make it. The other would be attacked by Steve. He'd be the tornado and make faces and wind noises. He said if we looked at him we'd turn to stone and die. We closed our eyes but he tried to pry them open. When the game ended, we were either crying or laughing.

"He made us scared of our toys," says Sue. He would come into her room and play Barbie dolls with her by staging a car crash. Or pretending that Barbie had come to life.

The worst happened when their parents went out and Steven baby-sat. "When he was baby-sitting for us," says Sue, "he'd resort to creative torture. One time he came into the bedroom with his face wrapped in toilet paper like a mummy. He peeled off the paper layer by layer and threw it at us. He was a delight, but a terror. And we kept coming back for more."

"Steven was King Bee with his sisters," says Leah.

"He had control over the whole house," says Anne.

"Here he was, the only boy in the family," says Sue. "He was definitely king of the family."

And Nancy adds, "He had his own agenda. There were two types of torture—mental and physical."

But things changed as Anne grew older. She and Steve became partners. "First he tortured me," she says. "Then *we* tortured *them*."

Sue and Steven would get into terrible fights. "He would push me and I would scratch him," she says. "He would do that thing where he held my head with his long arm and I'd be trying to punch him. At one point he would scream, 'Anne! Quick! She's hysterical!' And that was Anne's cue to run to the kitchen and get a glass of water and he'd throw it in my face. So that was how the fights would usually end."

"*Poltergeist,*" said Steven, "is about all the terrible things I did to my sisters. From seven to thiry-three I was really awful to them."

Sue, baby Nancy, and Anne, *above.* The Spielberg family at home in New Jersey, *opposite page. Clockwise from top left:* Arnold, Philip Posner holding Nancy, Jennie Posner, Leah, Steven's uncle Bernard Posner, Anne, Steven, and Sue.

"*Poltergeist* is about all the terrible things I did to my younger sisters. From seven to thirty-three I was really awful to them."

The Last Shootout

"I've always considered Arizona, where I was from nine to sixteen, my real home," wrote Steven in an autobiographical piece. "For a kid, home is where you have your best friends and your first car, and your first kiss; it's where you do your worst stuff and get your best grades."

In February 1957, Steven's family moved from New Jersey to Phoenix, Arizona. Arnold had a new job with General Electric. The family settled in the suburbs and lived in a one-story ranch style house. "You saw my house when you saw *Close Encounters*, *Poltergeist*, and *E.T.*," Steven said.

"We had a long narrow hallway where the four bedrooms were," remembers Sue. "If we walked by Steven and he was walking in the opposite direction, we'd have to flatten up against the wall."

"His room was a private sanctuary," says Anne. "No one went in without being invited. It also was rarely clean."

"It was so filthy," says his mother, "I wouldn't go in."

Steven was prepared for any assault on his privacy. "He had a fake rubber snake in his closet," says Sue. "When the housekeeper went in to open his closet to put some clothes away, it fell on her and she ran screaming down the hall."

The family had a pet dog, a buff cocker spaniel named Thunder. Steven also had pet parakeets in his

The Spielberg family in Arizona, *top*. Anne, Sue, and Steven, *bottom*.

room, but he wouldn't keep them in cages. "They flew free form," says Leah. "I like them—*outside*. There were a couple of times that the cocker spaniel ate a couple of his birds."

Shortly after the move to Phoenix, Leah gave her husband an 8mm Brownie movie camera. "It was a real cheap, no-frills camera," Arnold recalls. "You couldn't even focus it—it was a fixed-focus camera." The family often went camping on the weekend in the Arizona White Mountains. "My dad would take the camera along and film the trips," Steven said in an interview, "and we'd sit down and watch the footage a week later. It would put me right to sleep."

When Steven kept criticizing his father's home movies, Arnold said, "If you know so much, why don't you try?" And he handed over the camera.

"I became the family photographer," said Steven, "and logged all our trips. I was fascinated. I had the power of choice.

"Then I began to think that staging real life was much more exciting than just recording it. So I'd do things like forcing my parents to let me out of the car a hundred yards before we reached the campgrounds when we went on trips. I'd run ahead and film them arriving and unpacking and pitching camp."

Occasionally Leah and Arnold went away by themselves. Once, when they were going on a vacation, Steven wanted to take a shot of the camper pulling out of the driveway. "He got down on his belly and was aiming at the hubcap," Leah remembers. "We were exasperated, yelling at him, 'Come on! We have to leave! Hurry up!' But he just kept on doing his thing, and when we saw the finished results, he was able to pull back so that this hubcap spinning around became the whole camper—my first glimpse at the Spielbergian touch and a hint of things to come."

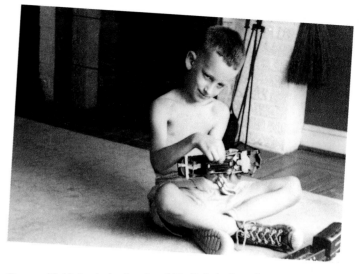

Steven with his toy train, the star of his first short movie.

Steven made his first short movie, *The Last Train Wreck*, when he was eleven. (The impact of *The Greatest Show on Earth* continued.) The movie was three minutes long and showed his toy electric trains crashing into each other. "I used to love to stage little wrecks," said Steven. "My dad said, 'If you break your trains one more time I'll take them away!' So I took his camera and staged a great train wreck....Then I could look at my 8mm film over and over and enjoy the demolition of my trains without the threat of losing them."

Steven made his first film with a real story line when he was twelve so that he could earn a Boy Scout merit badge. Although Steven was an enthusiastic Boy Scout, he later admitted he "was always doing doofy things" such as dropping his mess kit in the mud and cutting his knuckle while demonstrating ax sharpening in front of five hundred scouts.

Once, after building a campfire, he was so tired and hungry that he forgot to open a can of beans before putting it into a pot of boiling water. It exploded. Shrapnel flew in all directions. "No one was hurt," he says, "but everyone within twenty yards of the fire needed new uniforms."

Steven did not do well at sports. "My worst subject was phys ed," he wrote later. "I couldn't do a chin-up." Yet he wanted to become an Eagle Scout. Then, as now, this involved earning twenty-one merit badges. "A merit badge is an accomplishment in a field," explains Arnold, who trained as a scoutmaster. "There are about sixty or seventy different fields—nature study, boating, gymnastics. But Steve was not an athletic kid." Steven scraped through with swimming, canoeing, and completing an obstacle course, barely earning his merit badges.

However, Steven was good at one thing—telling stories. "I used to sit around the campfire and scare forty scouts to death with ghost stories," he says.

"He was making amateur movies at that time," remembers Arnold, "but there wasn't a movie merit badge. So the scoutmaster said, 'You go out and make a movie, and if it's good, we'll just give you a merit badge for it.'" Arnold gave Steven the Brownie movie camera and three rolls of film, and he went out in the desert and made a Western.

Steven filmed it at a restaurant called Pinnacle Peak Patio, in Scottsdale, Arizona. "He had an old stagecoach without wheels just standing there," recalls Anne, "and I was the passenger in the stagecoach. I had my jewelry box. And the bad guys came with the bandannas and cap pistols out and robbed me. And I think killed the driver and took my jewelry. Of course they spilled it all over the desert. I never found all of it."

Steven has referred to the movie as *The Last Gunfight*, *The Last Gun*, and *The Last Shootout*.

"It was the neatest little movie!" says Arnold proudly. "We had no editing equipment, nothing you could use to cut the movie with, so he edited it in the

Leah, *above*, and Sue in Western gear.

camera. Like when he had a gunfight he had one guy reach for his gun and stop. Then he'd turn to the other fella and say, 'Now reach for your gun.' And it came out in sequence like that. He just had that kind of instinct for doing things."

When Steven showed the movie to his troop at the next Monday night meeting, the Boy Scouts cheered, laughed, and applauded. "I really wanted to do that, to please again," said Steven.

He was given his merit badge and was the first member of his troop to become an Eagle Scout. Years later, "They created a new badge in honor of Steve," says Nancy—the cinematography merit badge.

out and got him a movie camera with a three-turret lens—a standard lens, a wide-angle lens, and a telephoto lens. "With that camera he started making a lot of movies," Arnold recalls. "Particularly war movies. He grabbed my bomber jacket, air force goggles, and every piece of equipment that I had."

Steven was inspired by stories his father told him about his experiences during World War II as a radio operator on a B-25 bomber. Many years later, these same stories would inspire *Saving Private Ryan*. Steven began filming *Fighter Squad* when he was thirteen years old and in seventh grade. Some of the boys he knew acted as pilots. But he wanted to use a real plane.

"There were some P-51s at the Phoenix airport," says Arnold. "I took him there and he asked if we could use one of the planes." After they got permission, "Steven put a kid wearing a helmet in the cockpit, and he sat on the nose of the plane taking pictures into the cockpit of the kid pretending to fly. We wanted to show the plane banking," says Arnold, "so he'd turn the camera. When it came out, it looked just like it! Then when he wanted to show *real* flight, he bought these little 8mm shorts of flying planes and he'd splice them in. It all matched."

Steven himself appeared in the movie. Jim Sollenberger, one of the other kids who acted in *Fighter Squad*, says, "Spielberg played a German—there were *always* Germans in Spielberg's pictures." In one scene Steven got shot and slumped over with food coloring coming out of his mouth like blood. Jim filmed it. He stood on the wing and tilted the camera sideways to make it look as though the front end of the plane was going down.

To earn money for film and equipment, Steven showed movies at home in the family room.

"He would print up tickets," remembers Leah, "and

Steven Spielberg, Eagle Scout.

(In recent years, the Boy Scouts of America has instituted a policy of barring homosexuals from participating in its activities. Steven has spoken out against this policy, while he still commends scouting as a good experience for boys. "I encourage—for the good of scouting—efforts to end this intolerance and discrimination once and for all," Steven has written.)

"Scouting gave me my start," Steven said. "From age twelve or thirteen I knew I wanted to be a movie director."

After finishing his Western, Steven realized that he needed a better camera. He returned the Brownie to Arnold and said, "Get me a good one, Dad." Arnold went send his sisters out on the hot summer's day while he's in the cool bedroom, to sell tickets door-to-door. Everybody wanted to come to our house."

"Growing up in Arizona," says Nancy, "there was very little to do. Nobody went to camp. We could either go to the library or play in the sprinklers. It was *so* hot. You just couldn't go outside and play."

"We were known in the neighborhood," says Sue. "The kids would gather on Sunday on warm summer nights."

"He'd rent movies and put a sheet up," says Anne.

"Movies were projector movies in those days," adds Sue. "There were no videos."

"I'd bring home the company projector," recalls Arnold, "and he would rent a feature film at a store for fifteen dollars and then he would show that as the primary feature, then his stuff as shorts. He made a big cardboard cutout and put the projector behind and cut a hole in it so you wouldn't hear the sound of the projector, and I'd set up the speakers for him. And the kids would sell candy at the door."

"I ran the concession stand," says Anne. "I popped popcorn and put it in brown paper bags."

But Arnold told Steven, "'You can't keep the money for the admission price because that's a commercial picture.' So he would donate it to the Perry Institute. And he would keep the candy money to buy film, pay off his sisters a little bit, and keep going. *And* he would get written up in the newspaper!"

Steven received more attention from the press when he made one of his next war movies, *Escape to Nowhere*. The movie was based on World War II German field marshal Erwin Rommel's corps fighting American troops in the North African desert. Steven filmed it in the desert around Camelback Mountain in Phoenix. Leah loaned Steven her army surplus jeep for the movie.

"I put on my army fatigues," recalls Arnold, "and I'd crunch down and drive the jeep, leading a column of American soldiers through the desert." Leah also drove the jeep in some of the scenes, wearing a helmet over her short blond hair while playing the part of a German soldier.

About twenty or thirty boys performed in the battle scenes. But they had to double as Germans and Americans to make the cast seem larger. Since Steven only had a few German helmets, he had the boys run past the camera, then pass their helmets on to the next kids. Even Anne became part of the cast. "We were shy a soldier the day we filmed the scene," Steve told a reporter for the *Arizona Republic* who was covering the making of the movie, "so we had her put on a uniform and helmet and got rid of her in a hurry, wearing a German uniform and crawling on her stomach."

"Steve cooked up special effects," says Arnold.

"My special effects were great," boasted Steven. Arnold helped him figure out how to create the illusion of explosions, and with his knowledge of chemistry, also made fireworks.

Steven completed the movie when he was sixteen and entered it in the Arizona Amateur Film Festival Contest. He won first prize. "His prize," recalls Arnold, "was a 16mm movie camera, a Kodak, and a bunch of books on photography and moviemaking. He donated all the books to the high-school library," because he didn't think he needed them.

Steven at about sixteen

"'Steve,'" said Arnold, "'I can't afford to buy 16mm film. Let's trade this in for an 8mm camera.'" So Arnold went to a camera store and got Steven a good Bolex 8mm movie camera and a sound system. "They had just come out with 8mm sound," says Arnold. "It was crude but it worked." For the first time, Steven was able to record sound. He used this equipment for his next venture, *Firelight*.

Meanwhile, he was doing poorly in school. Steven did not enjoy reading as much as watching television, going to movies, and making his own films. The only things he really liked to read were science-fiction stories, *Mad* magazine, and film magazines. Although Arnold enthusiastically helped him with his productions, he still hoped that Steve would eventually become an electrical engineer. He woke Steven up early each morning and tutored him in math.

But it was hopeless. "I hated math," said Steven. When he counted on his fingers, his father would look away. "I still can't do a fraction," Steven said in a recent interview. He remained a C student all through high school.

The conflict between Steven and Arnold over schoolwork created a distance between them. But there were other tensions in the household. Leah and Arnold were not getting along. At night Steven and his sisters huddled together, listening to their parents arguing and saying the *D* word. "For years, I thought the word 'divorce' was the ugliest in the English language," said Steven. The troubles at home, as well as the good times, affected him deeply and had a lasting influence on his work.

In 1964, as Steven was entering his senior year of high school, Arnold accepted a new job with IBM. The whole family went with him to Saratoga in Northern California. Steven expressed the pain of moving, "the good-bye scene," as he called it, in his movie *E.T.* "All my friends would be there and we'd say good-bye to each other and I would leave," he said in an interview. "This happened to me four major times in my life. And the older I got the harder it got."

A Boy's Life

The summer before Steven began his senior year at Saratoga High School, he worked as a clerical assistant in the editorial department of Universal Pictures. Although he was not paid, the job enabled him to roam around the lot and learn about professional filmmaking. "I visited every set I could, got to know people, observed techniques, and just generally absorbed the atmosphere," Steven said.

He landed the job through his contact with Chuck Silvers, head librarian at Universal Pictures. Steven had met Silvers the previous summer when he was visiting Los Angeles: He had taken a tram ride tour of Universal Studios.

"The tram wasn't stopping at the sound stages," wrote Steven in an autobiographical piece for *Time* magazine. "So during a bathroom break I snuck away and wandered over there, just watching. I met a man who asked what I was doing and I told him my story. Instead of calling the guards to throw me off the lot he talked with me for about an hour. His name was Chuck Silvers. He said he'd like to see some of my little films, and so he gave me a pass to get on the lot the next day. I showed him about four of my 8mm films. He was very impressed."

Silvers remembers the day he met Steven. He was amazed when he heard about the seventeen-year-old's accomplishments—*Escape to Nowhere* and *Firelight*.

Steven as a teenager, *top*.
Nancy, Leah, and Sue, *bottom*.

And he was struck by Steven's excitement when they walked onto a dubbing stage. "It dawned on me that I was talking to somebody who had a burning ambition, and not only that, he was going to accomplish his mission," said Silvers. "I knew he was gonna do *something*." Silvers became Steven's mentor at Universal.

When the summer ended, Steven returned home and started school. He described his senior year at Saratoga High School as "hell on earth." For the first time he encountered anti-Semitism. Kids called him names, threw pennies at him, coughed "Jew" into their hands when they passed him, and even hit him.

"The idea that a person would hit me because I was Jewish was startling to me," he told interviewers later. "I felt as alien as I had ever felt in my life. It caused me great fear and an equal amount of shame."

Steven desperately wanted to belong, to look gentile so that he would be accepted. "At school I felt like a real nerd," he said. His nose bothered him most of all. At home, in the privacy of his bedroom, he would take a piece of duct tape and tape the tip of his nose to the top of his forehead to make it turn up. "I had this big nose," he said. "My face grew into it."

The year in Saratoga was also difficult for Steven and his whole family because of problems at home. "There were some very sad times there," says Sue. "It was very hard to see my parents' marriage falling apart."

Arnold, a workaholic and perfectionist, spent long hours at his job and often traveled. Leah, a stay-at-home mom, was more playful and artistic. "My mom and dad were so different," said Steven. "They both love classical music and they both love my sisters and me. Aside from that, they had nothing in common." In the evening, for instance, Leah, a pianist, performed chamber music with her friends in one room, while Arnold discussed computers with his friends in another room.

Late at night when Steven and his sisters heard their parents arguing, the girls would burst into tears, "and we would all hold one another," Steven recalled.

Leah and Arnold decided to separate at the end of the school year. "They hung in there to protect us until we were old enough," said Steven. "But I don't think they were aware of how acutely we were aware of their unhappiness—not violence, just a pervading unhappiness you could cut with a fork or a spoon at dinner every night."

Steven's parents—two bright, caring people—tried to do their best for their children. Yet Steven and his

> "I felt as alien as I had ever felt in my life. It caused me great fear and an equal amount of shame."

sisters suffered. "Sometimes parents can work together to raise a wonderful family and not have anything in common with each other," wrote Steven. "That happens a lot in America."

As he had since childhood, Steven continued to make films despite the conflict at home. One of them featured Thunder, the family's cocker spaniel. "Steven wanted to do a film, *This Is a Dog's Life*," said Sue. "It was all going to be filmed from the dog's point of view. I was in fifth or sixth grade. Nancy and I were fighting over which one of us was going to be the star. If he was mad at me, Nancy was going to be the star. And if he was mad at Nancy, vice-versa."

Steven's script called for the girls to find the dog on a dark, rainy night. "He took our poor white cocker spaniel outside," recalls Sue, "and threw mud all over him, and we were supposed to carry this dog in and give him a bath. Our mom let us do this, with her beautiful floors and carpeting!"

Steven also filmed high-school football games, and a gag documentary about the senior class outing to Santa Cruz, a beach town nearby. But that year he concentrated more on schoolwork than he had before and tried to get decent grades.

However, when he applied to film school at the University of Southern California and the University of California at Los Angeles, they both turned him down because his grades were too low. Chuck Silvers put in a good word for him, to no avail. So Steven went to California State College at Long Beach (CSLB). Although the college didn't have a film department yet, it was close to Los Angeles and Universal Studios. And Steven planned to continue hanging out at Universal.

Around the time of his high-school graduation in June 1965, his parents announced they were going to get a divorce. "When my mom told us the news," recalls Sue, "she sat us down on the floor in the kitchen."

"She told me first," says Anne, then fifteen years old, "to be there with her when she told the other kids."

Arnold moved out of the house and went to Los Angeles. "When my father left," Steven said, "I went from tormentor to protector with my family . . . I had to become the man of the house."

At first the girls stayed with Leah in Saratoga. That summer Steven went to Los Angeles to live with his dad and commute to college. A year later Leah and the girls returned to Phoenix, and Leah married Bernie Adler, a close friend of the family, in 1967.

Years later Steven made a movie, *E.T.*, about his experiences in Saratoga. The original title of the movie was *A Boy's Life*. "*E.T.* is a very personal story . . . about the divorce of my parents," he said, "how I felt when my parents broke up." The movie was autobiographical in another way. Steven intended it as a "story about an ugly duckling, someone who didn't belong." He said, "I always felt *E.T.* was a minority story... that stands for every minority in this country."

Leah (right), Sue (center), and an unidentified friend (left) at the San Diego Zoo, *top*. Leah (center), Sue (center right), and Anne (far right) at a family gathering, *bottom*. Elliott (Henry Thomas) saving E. T., *opposite page*.

"*E.T.* is a very personal story . . . about the divorce of my parents, how I felt when my parents broke up."

Amblin'

Steven still liked watching and making movies more than going to classes. He spent two days a week at California State Long Beach and the other three on the studio lot at Universal. Knowing that Steven was indifferent to school, his father called Chuck Silvers at Universal and asked him to make sure that Steven attended classes so that he could earn his degree. But Silvers said, "For Steven to realize his ambitions he's going to need a hell of a big break. They don't care whether he's got a degree or not. They're interested in what he can put on screen."

Despite his disinterest in school, Steven was an excellent writer. "He had all these stories running through his head," recalls one of his professors, "and he was always jotting down little story ideas."

Steven hoped to get the top executives at Universal to see his films and give him a contract. "I wanted to be a director," he said. However, the executives wouldn't even take a look. "They said, 'If you make your films in 16mm, or even better, 35mm, then they'll get seen.'"

Even in college, Steven had continued working with his 8mm sound camera. Film size is given in millimeters. Wider film produces a sharper image, and professional movies all over the world are shot on 35mm film. Steven knew he needed to make a "showcase film" in order to be

The Universal studio lot, about the time Steven spent so much time there.

taken seriously. So he got a job working in the college cafeteria and earned enough money to rent a 16mm camera and buy film.

On weekends he shot experimental movies. Ralph Burris, a fellow English major, and other friends at CSLB performed in Steven's films. One of his professors said about Steven: "The kid was absolutely captivated by motion pictures. I never saw him without cameras hanging around his neck. He was always shooting film."

Steven's father worried about his son's lack of

interest in schoolwork. So did Steven's mother. Leah frequently called the chairman of the department of radio and television at CSLB to hear how Steven was doing and was upset to learn that he hardly paid attention to most of his classes.

Tensions mounted between Steven and his father. Finally Steven moved out of his dad's apartment and rented a place with Ralph Burris. Looking back, Steven said, "College could have helped me. If I'd paid more attention to college and less to motion-picture making, I might have delayed my career by a couple of years, but I think I would have had a much more well-rounded education."

On the lot at Universal Steven watched filmmakers such as Alfred Hitchcock at work, and had lunch with actors Charlton Heston and Cary Grant. He hung out in the cutting room and asked the editors a million questions. He became friends with a young actor, Tony Bill, who had appeared in *Come Blow Your Horn* with Frank Sinatra and who later became a producer and director. Bill took an interest in Steven's work.

Through him, Steven met another young filmmaker, Francis Ford Coppola. Bill also took Steven along to his acting class and introduced him to an actor and independent filmmaker, director John Cassavetes. Cassavetes invited Steven to work as a production assistant on a low-budget film he was making called *Faces*. Steven later said, "I got off on the right foot, learning about how to deal with actors as I watched Cassavetes dealing with his repertory company."

By 1967 Steven was ready to make his first 35mm film, a "calling card film" to demonstrate his talent as a filmmaker to the executives at Universal. He wrote a simple story about a bicycle race and called the project *Slipstream*. The word "slipstream" refers to the air current produced by and just behind a fast-moving vehicle. In Steven's movie the hero, played by Tony Bill, attempts to

win a bicycle race by daring to ride in the slipstream of a truck. Meanwhile his rival tries to knock him off his bike.

Steven's roommate Ralph was a student in law school by then. But Ralph dropped out to put up some of the money for Steven's movie and launch his own career as a producer. Steven's dad, despite his misgivings about Steven's schoolwork, helped rent equipment such as a Chapman crane and a Mitchell 35mm camera, and paid some of the bills for the sound crew.

Steven asked a young cinematographer, Allen Daviau, who was making rock 'n' roll films for record companies, to be his cameraman. "I really didn't know 35mm equipment," says Daviau, "but I knew a cameraman, a French cameraman named Serge Haginere. Serge had a lot of experience in all kinds of film. He was over here trying to get started. I introduced Steven to Serge. Serge was director of photography on the film and I ran the B camera, the second camera running.

"On all these bicycle-racing things we'd roll two cameras. We had a wider shot and a tighter shot or different angles. This was shot entirely on weekends, in the desert principally and Santa Monica. We'd go out

Allen Daviau at work.

with people in Los Angeles who belonged to European-style racing clubs," recalls Daviau. "We shot all day long from sunrise to sunset.

"I photographed racers silhouetted against the rising sun. The problem Steven had," says Daviau, "was that he had to get a beginning and the ending to the film, the start and finish of the race. They were well over their budget even though we were using borrowed equipment."

After weeks of shooting, Steven found a very nice location in Santa Monica and scheduled the last weekend of filming. "But the problem was it didn't just rain, it *monsooned*!" recalls Daviau. "It was a tragedy. They were out of money. We had lots of exciting footage but there was no way to finish it." All the equipment—crane and camera—had to be returned. The professional grips who knew how to run the crane left because they could no longer be paid. "Steven was very, very let down about it," says Daviau, "and tried to get another short film going."

That film was *Amblin'*. The money for it came from a different source. Steven heard that another aspiring producer was willing to finance a short film. Steven went in for an interview and sold his concept. "We started shooting it on July fourth in 1968," remembers Daviau, the director of photography this time. Steven wrote and directed the film. There was no dialogue, only music. "Film for me is totally pictorial," Steven once said. "I like to tell stories through pictures."

Amblin' tells the story of a young man and woman around Steven's age at the time, twenty-one, who hitchhike from the desert to the ocean in Southern California, fall in love, and ultimately drift apart. Most of the movie was filmed in Pearblossom, north of Los Angeles.

"It was a hundred and five degrees in July in Pearblossom," Daviau recalled. "It was not meant for

Shooting *Amblin'*. Anne Spielberg is holding the marker at right.

human beings to be out there with film cameras." But Steven's friends and family still believed in him despite the *Slipstream* disaster, and they all helped with the project. For the final sequence, Steven borrowed a friend's beach house in Malibu. Ralph took charge of production.

Steven's sister Anne was the script supervisor and the caterer. "I was in charge of continuity," she said, "and also in charge of breakfast and lunch for all the crew and cast. I would make sandwiches in the trailer.

"*Amblin'* was something he wrote very quickly," said Anne. "Steven dictated the script to me." Everyone, including Steven, worked on *Amblin'* for nothing except screen credit. It was a showcase film for cast and crew.

"*Amblin'* was a conscious effort to break into the business and become successful by proving to people I could move a camera and compose nicely and deal with lighting and performances," said Steven. It didn't carry a personal meaning from childhood like many of his films. "The only challenge that's close to my heart about *Amblin'* is I was able to tell a story about a boy and a girl with no dialogue."

After Steven finished editing the film down to twenty-six minutes, and completing the soundtrack, he was ready to show it to Chuck Silvers. "When I saw *Amblin'*," recalls Silvers, "I cried. It was everything it should have been. It was perfect." Silvers showed the movie to three or four other editors to get their reaction, and they all felt the same way. "It was pretty obvious," said Silvers, "that television was the way to go for Steven."

Although Steven hoped to make feature films for theaters he wanted to break into the field any way he

Steven and Sidney J. Sheinberg.

Amblin' "had a tremendous amount of heart and sensitivity to it, and I really thought it was quite terrific."—*Sidney J. Sheinberg*

could and become a professional. So on a rainy night in fall 1968, Silvers called Sidney J. Sheinberg, president of Universal TV. Silvers recalls telling Sheinberg, "I have a twenty-six-minute film here that you must see. You've got to see it tonight because someone else is liable to see it tomorrow." Sheinberg saw the movie and later recalled, "It had a tremendous amount of heart and sensitivity to it, and I really thought it was quite terrific."

He met with Steven, and a week later Steven signed a seven-year contract with Universal to direct television shows and maybe movies. "I quit college so fast," said Steven, "I didn't even clean out my locker."

As soon as Steven told Silvers the good news about his contract, he asked what he could do to say thank you. "I want two things," said Silvers. "I want you to help, in any way you can, young people like yourself." Steven promised he would. Then he asked, "What's the other thing?"

"Whenever we meet, I want a hug."

Twenty-six years later Silvers says, "He kept his word. Every time I see Steven I get my hug."

Duel and *The Sugarland Express*

"I began directing a year shy of graduation," Steven said, "which my father will *never* forgive me for."

Steven's first assignment at Universal Pictures was to direct an episode of *Night Gallery*, a TV show written and hosted by Rod Serling. The episode was called "Eyes" and starred Joan Crawford, a leading Hollywood movie actress since the 1920s. Steven was terrified. "That's when the cold sweat began," he later recalled. He was twenty-one, she was sixty-three. Before meeting Crawford, he bought a book about her films and tried to memorize all the names and details. When he went to her apartment, she was astonished by how young he was.

"Goodness," she told him, "you certainly must have done something important to get where you are so soon."

She asked him what films he had directed and he replied, "None," except the twenty-six-minute short he had made at school. Then she asked him if he was the son of any of the top executives at Universal.

"No, ma'am," he said, "I'm just working my way through Universal." His answer amused Crawford, and according to her biographer Bob Thomas, they went out to dinner. Or did they? In true Hollywood style, there is another account of their first meeting. In this one, Joan Crawford didn't go out to dinner with Steven at all. "I don't want you sitting with me in a restaurant," she is said to have told him. "People will think you're my son, not my director."

Steven began shooting "Eyes" on February 3, 1969. "I was so frightened that even now the whole period is a bit of a blank. I was walking on eggs." To Steven's surprise, Crawford treated him with respect. "She was terrific, totally professional," he said. "She relied on me to direct her more than I ever thought she would."

"There are some pictures of Steven and Joan Crawford," recalls Steven's mother. "In one picture Joan Crawford is sitting in a chair. Steve is kneeling, and her face watching Steve says it all. She was in absolute awe of him. When she first heard this *pisher* kid [*pisher* in Yiddish means an inexperienced young person] was going to direct her, she said, 'No way, no way.' And then

Steven directing Joan Crawford, *opposite page.*

"She relied on me to direct her."

they met and she adored Steve. They were very good friends."

The crew thought Steven had been hired as a publicity stunt. "I came on the set and they thought it was a joke," he recalled. "I really couldn't get anybody to take me seriously. It was very embarrassing."

Undaunted, Steven took charge. He had done his homework and prepared for filming by making storyboards, which are drawings of all the scenes in sequence. "I had my storyboards right there with me every minute," he said. In this way he could visualize the whole film. The story, set in New York, tells of a wealthy blind woman (played by Crawford) who blackmails a surgeon into removing the eyes of a poor

---

"I came on the set and they thought it was a joke."

---

gambler and transplanting them into her so that she can see for a few hours. Just as the bandages are removed, there's a blackout in New York, and the woman sees nothing except darkness. Horrified by what she has done—for nothing—she goes insane. Steven thought the script was terrible, but he dreamed up some imaginative camera angles to make it more interesting.

"Eyes" aired on NBC on November 8, 1969, and received mixed reviews. One reporter wrote, "Steve Spielberg's direction of the Crawford seg is topnotch." But another critic slammed the episode for being too arty and put Steven down because of his age. The bad reviews bothered him. "All of a sudden the age factor began to plague me," he said.

During the next eight months, Steven received no other directing assignments at Universal. He took an informal leave of absence and concentrated on writing instead. What he really wanted to do was to make original movies for TV or Hollywood. He tried to sell some of his scripts to studios other than Universal, but everyone turned him down. Finally he went back to Universal and directed more television shows. Over the next seven years, Steven directed episodes of many TV shows, including *Marcus Welby, M.D.*, and *Columbo*.

"TV for me wasn't an art form, it was a job," Steven said, looking back. "Because of television I didn't know for a while whether or not I wanted to continue making film . . . I wasn't getting any of that stimulation, that gratification that I even got making 8mm war movies when I was twelve years old. I didn't have that passion . . . It's only when I got into feature films—actually when I got into TV movies and made *Duel*—that I kind of rediscovered the fun about making films."

Duel, a story by science-fiction writer Richard Matheson, first appeared in *Playboy* magazine. "I was just knocked out by it. And I wanted to make it into a feature film," said Steven. The story told of a driver terrorized by a trucker trying to bump him off the road as they chase along miles and miles of California highway. "The truck itself becomes a monster," wrote Stephen King.

Universal bought the film rights for the story, and Matheson developed a script with the producer. Steven persuaded the producer to let him direct it.

Cameras rolled on September 13, 1971, in the desert near Lancaster and Palmdale where Steven had filmed *Amblin'*. Again he made storyboards. First he did the drawings himself with stick figures. Then, he said, "I had an artist paint an entire map, as if a helicopter camera had photographed the entire road where the

David Mann (Dennis Weaver) in the driver's seat in *Duel* (top) and his enemy, the truck (bottom), *opposite page.*

"The truck itself becomes a monster." —*Stephen King*

chase was taking place. And then that entire map had little sentences—like, 'This is where the car passes the truck,' or 'This is where the truck passes the car and then the car passes the truck.' And I was able to wrap this map around the motel room, and I just crossed things off—until the entire map was shot," he said.

For the truck, Steven found a beat-up gasoline tanker that looked almost human. "I put dead bugs all over the windshield," he said, "so you'd have a tougher time seeing the driver." He created suspense by never showing the driver of the truck, only his arm signaling out the window and his cowboy boots. Actor Dennis Weaver played the part of David Mann, who drives the car and ultimately wins the duel by forcing the truck over a cliff.

The movie aired on Saturday night, November 13, 1971, as an ABC Movie of the Weekend. It received rave reviews. *Los Angeles Times* critic Cecil Smith praised Steven as "the *wunderkind* of the film business." Another young filmmaker, George Lucas, who had met Steven a couple of times, was at a party at Francis Ford Coppola's house, and sneaked upstairs to catch a few minutes of *Duel*. "Once I started watching," Lucas recalled later, "I couldn't tear myself away. I thought, this guy is really sharp. I've got to get to know him better."

An expanded version of *Duel* was released in Europe at movie theaters and established Steven's reputation internationally. Director David Lean, one of Steven's idols, who had made *The Bridge on the River Kwai* and *Lawrence of Arabia*, saw *Duel* in London. "Immediately I knew that here was a very bright new director," Lean said.

With the success of *Duel* Steven achieved a new status as a hot director. More than ever he longed to break out of television and do a feature film. He had worked on a script idea for a movie based on an incident he had read about in the newspaper. The article told of an ex-convict

in Texas and his wife who took a highway patrolman hostage and led the police on a high-speed chase as they tried to reach their children. In Steven's adaptation, the husband and wife have escaped from jail and are on the run trying to rescue their little boy from his foster home. Steven developed the script with two screenwriters, Hal Barwood and Matthew Robbins, and in April 1972, they received the go-ahead from Universal. The project was called *The Sugarland Express*, after the fictional town in Texas where the couple ends up.

For the part of the young mother, Steven chose actress Goldie Hawn. Although she had won an Oscar as

Steven—the *wunderkind* of the film business, *above*. Making forty police cars look like a hundred in *The Sugarland Express, opposite page*. Goldie Hawn and William Atherton (later in *Die Hard*) played the young parents.

"Our budget only allowed us forty police cars, but I had to make it look like a hundred."

Steven preparing for his later road movies.

and rented seventeen others from the Texas Department of Public Safety.

Since this was a road movie like *Duel*, Steven had a graphic artist make a mural showing the progress of the chase. He also had storyboards drawn. "I had the art department build a miniature used car lot from cardboard and [Matchbox] toys," he said. "It's a lot simpler to shuffle around toys in a six-foot layout than to try to move the real thing. Then from this mock-up I chose all of my angles.

"I always had a visual overview in terms of day-to-day scheduling," he said. Yet Steven didn't want to be overprepared. "Marvelous accidents happen on the set—actors have suggestions, technicians have suggestions, a passing stranger might have a suggestion—and I think a director should keep his mind open every day and not get trapped by the kind of homework he falls in love with on the eve of shooting the actual scene."

Steven and his cinematographer, Vilmos Zsigmond,

"Marvelous accidents happen on the set."

Best Supporting Actress for *Cactus Flower* in 1969, she was then known not for her dramatic roles, but for playing a ditzy blonde on TV's *Laugh-In*. The theme of a child's separation from his parents and the desperate need to reconnect echoed Steven's painful feelings about his parents' divorce and the breakup of his family.

Another element that sprang from Steven's childhood was his excitement at staging the biggest car chase ever put on film, ending in spectacular crashes. In the true story about ninety police cars chased after the young couple. "Our budget only allowed us forty police cars," said Steven, "but I had to make it look like a hundred." His unit production manager, Bill Gilmore, bought twenty-three cars at a police auction

discussed ways of filming the action with natural light to make the movie look as much as possible like a documentary. They set up a track on a platform so that they could shoot film alongside the cars in motion. "I don't know where Steven got the ideas he tried to do, because I had never seen shots like that," said Zsigmond. "Steven realizes the moving camera is essential for movies."

"I went [on location in San Antonio, Texas] for two

weeks to be there for his first feature," Anne said. "There's a scene where all the police cars suddenly take off. And they do it from a chicken take-out place. There's a big revolving chicken on top. There were maybe fifteen or twenty police cars with their lights going.

"Steve was on the roof of the chicken place directing the scene with a camera up there so he has this one angle as the cars go by. And I just remember being on the ground looking up at him as these cars all took off with the sirens and lights going into the sunset. Our eyes met and it was, 'Yeah! This is what we've been doing! This is what it is! This is fantastic! I'm doing something I love!'" Steven brought back the revolving neon chicken sign as a souvenir and put it in his office at Universal.

The Sugarland Express marked the beginning of his collaboration with John Williams, who composed the score.

"Among the first things Steven did was to say, 'I remember your score from such and such a movie,'" recalled Williams. "And he would sing the third subordinate theme of Aunt Sarah's character in some film I had forgotten I did. And he remembered it all, as he still does."

Steven had always loved film scores, and he collected hundreds of soundtracks. "Steve had *every* soundtrack from *every* motion picture," said his sister Sue. As children he and Anne played a game called Needle Drop or Name That Tune. One of them would stay in the den, and the other in the living room with louvered doors in between.

"I'd put the needle down on the record," says Anne, "and after three or four notes pick it up and say, 'Name that movie.' He was very good. After a couple notes, he got it. Then it would be my turn."

Steven's total recall of movie music greatly impressed John Williams, who at the age of forty-one had been in the business for fourteen years. He

> "Our eyes met and it was, 'This is fantastic! I'm doing something I love!'"
>
> —Anne Spielberg

described Steven as having "tremendous retention, tremendous energy, youth and vitality and all that, and sweetness."

The Sugarland Express opened on April 5, 1974, and received outstanding reviews. Esteemed critic Pauline Kael of the *New Yorker* wrote, "This is one of the most phenomenal debut films in the history of movies."

Despite the reviews, the movie flopped at the box office. Audiences stayed away in droves. And those who saw it were shocked by the tragic ending. People expected a comedy from Goldie Hawn.

Steven heard the bad news at Martha's Vineyard as he started work on another movie—a story about a shark. With his next film, he vowed, he would hook the audience.

Jaws

"*Jaws* is a horror story about the great white shark," Steven said. "Unlike the dolphin, it doesn't speak; it just chows down."

The movie *Jaws* starts with a scene at night on the beach. Some college students sit around a campfire, playing guitars and partying. One of the girls jumps up and runs toward the ocean to go skinny-dipping. A boy stumbles after her. She plunges into the moonlit surf by herself and swims toward a buoy. An underwater view shows her swimming in the dark. Low, menacing music is heard. The camera cuts to a close-up of the girl's face. Something beneath the surface jerks her. She gurgles. Screams. Her body is yanked back and forth, then pulled furiously through the water. She screams for help. No one hears.

"I'm not so much afraid of sharks," Steven said. "I'm afraid of the water. And I'm afraid of everything that exists underneath the water that I can't see."

In 1973 Steven read a prepublication copy of *Jaws*, a novel by Peter Benchley. The story told of a great white shark that terrorizes a beach community off the coast of Long Island. "It terrified me," said Steven, "and I wanted to strike back. Fear is a very real thing for me. One of the best ways to cope with it is to turn it around and put it out to others. I mean, if you are afraid of the dark, you put the audience in a dark theater. I had a great fear of the ocean."

Universal wanted to buy the rights to film the book, and after a fierce bidding contest with other studios, it won. At first studio heads thought they would give the project to a more experienced director. But Steven expressed tremendous interest in *Jaws*, and the studio finally selected him. "The kid can bring visual excitement to it," said the producers, Richard Zanuck and David Brown.

Benchley wrote two screenplays based on his novel, but Steven wasn't satisfied, so he hired a friend, screenwriter Carl Gottlieb, to rewrite the script with him.

Steven asked actor Richard Dreyfuss to play the part of Matt Hooper, the shark expert who joins in the hunt for the great white. "He told me a very exciting story," recalls Dreyfuss. "But I said, 'No! No! I'd rather watch this movie than shoot it.'" Dreyfuss changed his mind, though, after he saw a film he had just completed and hated his own performance. "I begged for the job the week *Jaws* was starting to shoot," remembers Dreyfuss, "and he gave it to me."

When cameras rolled on May 2, 1974, the script wasn't ready. "We started that movie without a script,

"I thought that what could really be scary was *not* seeing the shark."

STEVEN SPIELBERG

without a cast, and without a shark," said Dreyfuss. Steven and Gottlieb shared a house on Martha's Vineyard, and every night they rewrote pages of script in preparation for the next day's shooting. The actors helped by improvising lines.

"Steven led this group of us," remembers Dreyfuss. "We talked about it, sketched it out, and created a scene every day, every night, for four months. It was a very intense experience, the most intense experience of all the films I've ever done. I learned the most, I changed the most. I did research, lots of homework. Shooting on the island we knew more about sharks than most people."

From the start, the project posed enormous production problems. Many times Steven thought of quitting. "I believe that summer was the most important summer in Steve's life," says Dreyfuss. "He was faced with a truly tremendous amount of pressure and demands."

First of all, Steven insisted that *Jaws* be filmed in the ocean rather than in a tank of water on the studio lot. "I wanted to shoot this in the ocean for reality," he said. But the weather changed greatly from day to day so it was hard to match the shots. For instance, if they started filming a scene outdoors on a sunny day and went back to finish the same scene the next day when it was dark and cloudy, the color of the sky looked different and the scene would not seem convincing to the audience. The cast and crew would have to wait for another sunny day to finish shooting.

Steven wanted to create the impression that his characters were out on the ocean by themselves fighting the man-eating shark. Unfortunately, many vacationers sailed by in their boats and refused to go away, creating more problems.

The shark itself was the biggest headache. Steven hired Bob Mattey, who had created a squid for Disney's

20,000 Leagues Under the Sea, to build a mechanical shark at Universal in Los Angeles. Mattey constructed three of them, collectively called Bruce, and they were delivered by truck to Martha's Vineyard. The first one sank, the second one exploded, and the third one didn't work. When Steven saw the first rushes (film that had been shot that day) of Bruce, his heart sank.

"Bruce's eyes crossed, and his jaws wouldn't close right," said Brian De Palma, a filmmaker friend visiting Steven on location.

"The shark was a disaster. It let us down tremendously," said the producer of the film, Richard Zanuck.

> ## "I believe that summer was the most important summer in Steve's life."
> —*Richard Dreyfuss*

Working frantically through the summer, Mattey and his crew upgraded the shark, and finally Bruce worked occasionally.

Meanwhile, Steven figured out a solution: He dramatically *suggested* the shark's presence rather than *showing* it. "I thought that what could really be scary was *not* seeing the shark," he said. He also used footage of real sharks that had been shot in Australia.

As a result of production problems, the shooting schedule ran way overtime and the budget doubled. Members of the cast and crew wanted to go home to their families or on to other jobs. They began calling the movie *Flaws* instead of *Jaws*.

"Four days out of seven we were making it, I thought it would be a turkey," said Steven.

"I thought my career as a filmmaker was over. I heard rumors from back in Hollywood that I would never work again because no one had ever taken a film a hundred days over schedule—let alone a director whose first picture had failed at the box office . . . There were moments of solitude, sitting on the boat waiting for a shot, thinking, 'This can't be done. It was stupid to begin it, we'll never finish it. No one is ever going to see this picture.'"

Steven's dad visited him on location and even appeared in a beach scene. "I saw Steven come out of the water after a day's shooting and lay down at the edge of the water, exhausted, just collapsed," Arnold remembers.

Steven (center) on location for *Jaws*.

The film's editor, Verna Fields, worked on *Jaws* during shooting on Martha's Vineyard, and later in post-production, back in Los Angeles. The job of the film editor is to suggest the sequence in which scenes and shots would appear to create different effects. Many critics praised her contributions as "saving" the final film. But Fields said that Steven "delivered so much good footage that it became an editor's dream."

An integral part of *Jaws* was the score, composed by John Williams. Before Williams even wrote the music, Steven imagined how it might sound. "Steven dragged me into his office [on Martha's Vineyard]," recalls Dreyfuss, and said, 'Want to hear the score? It isn't written yet, but...' And Steven played LP records, excerpts from Aaron Copland and Benjamin Britten. He was hearing something in his head."

Williams created the frightening theme to represent the shark. "I thought it was too primitive. I wanted something a little more melodic for the shark," Steven said when he first heard it. But he soon realized that Williams's theme was just right. The music scared audiences when they couldn't see the shark.

"*Jaws* was a good picture before it was scored, but the score did tremendous things for it," said Fields. She won an Oscar for Best Film Editing on *Jaws,* and Williams won his first Oscar for Best Original Score.

Today the shark's theme is used as a beach warning in Australia. "On the shore they play it if there's a shark in the water. And when people hear it, they get out!" says Richard Dreyfuss.

Steven added many personal touches to *Jaws*. He cast his cocker spaniel, Elmer, as Chief Brody's dog. And he gave Chief Brody, played by Roy Scheider, his own fear of the water. Brody has to overcome this phobia in order to go after the shark.

In one of the opening scenes, as Brody tries to warn the community about a shark attack, a group of Boy Scouts is out in the ocean doing a mile swim to earn their merit badges—just the way Steven did. Brody stands on the beach and scans the ocean. Is there a shark out there? The mood is threatening. Williams's ominous music comes up. Teenagers in the water scream. Suspense builds. At the water's edge Brody's little boy plays in the sand, oblivious to

Matt Hooper (Richard Dreyfuss) and Chief Brody (Roy Scheider) under attack, *left*. Beachgoers flee the great white shark.

impending danger, and sings, "Do you know the muf-fin man?"

"That was one of Steven's favorite childhood tunes," says his sister Sue.

"I saw *Jaws* with him the first time," says Steven's sister Anne. "It was at a special screening at the Cinerama Dome [in Los Angeles] for the distributors. We were sitting together and these guys, usually stone-faced, were going wild."

Dreyfuss attended the premiere of *Jaws* in New York. "At the end of the movie the audience gave

Steven a standing ovation," he says. "I had never heard an audience do that before. They were scream-ing, yelling, and applauded twice."

"For years he just scared us. Now he gets to scare the masses," says Anne.

Jaws broke all records at the box office. Two weeks after its release in June 1975, it became the most suc-cessful film in motion-picture history up to that time. At age twenty-eight, Steven was a millionaire. But the most important part of his success, says Anne, was "getting permission to do what he wanted to do."

Close Encounters

During filming of *Jaws* on Martha's Vineyard, Steven had discussed an idea for another movie with actor Richard Dreyfuss. "The more he told me, the more I saw real nobility in this one . . . A new concept, a benign view of life on other planets, a loving look. No one had done that, and I was bound and determined to be in that film," said Dreyfuss. Steven was considering other actors for the lead role in *Close Encounters of the Third Kind*, but Dreyfuss said to him, "'You need a man who is a child.' And he said, 'That's true. You've got the part.'"

The theme of *Close Encounters* is a naïve sense of wonder about the possibility of other worlds. "I really wanted to take a child's point of view," said Steven.

His story told of an ordinary family man (Dreyfuss), who encounters a UFO during a blackout. After the experience, Dreyfuss's character mysteriously knows that aliens will arrive in a mother ship. He is compelled to make contact with them. "A typical guy—nothing ever happens to him. Then, all of a sudden, he encounters something extraordinary and has to change his entire life in order to measure up to the task of either defeating it or understanding." It is one of Steven's favorite themes.

Meanwhile, in the film, a little boy (played by Cary Guffrey) wakes up one night as lights and shadows flicker across his face. The toys in his room start to move by themselves. A phonograph record begins to play. While his mother sleeps, the boy goes downstairs. The refrigerator opens, food spills onto the floor, and the doggy door bangs open and shut. The boy runs outside, laughing as UFOs fly overhead in a starry sky. But the toy cars have driven under his mother's bed and awakened her. She goes out looking for her son and snatches him up just as Dreyfuss's truck is about to hit him.

However, in a later scene, the UFOs fly directly over their house. An intense red light shines through the keyhole of the living-room door. The boy opens the door and faces a blinding orange-red light. Steven later selected this scene as a single image that summed up his work. The boy is "very small, and it's a large door, and there's a lot of promise or danger outside that door." An encounter of the first kind is the sighting of a UFO, the second is physical evidence that UFO and alien life exist, and the third is physical contact and communication with aliens, like the boy's. He crawls through the doggy door, following the light. His mother desperately tries to pull him inside. But he gets away. When she rushes outside, he's gone.

A little boy follows the light, *opposite page*.

"There's a lot of promise or danger outside that door."

Steven wrote the script himself over a two-year period, developing it from *Firelight*, the film he had made as a teenager. (The boy facing the blinding light is reminiscent of Steven's sister Nancy crawling toward the blinding firelight.) Production began in May 1976, with Columbia Pictures backing the project.

In the movie Dreyfuss quarrels with his wife over his growing obsession to reach a mountain that he believes will be the landing site of the aliens. He

Steven in front of the aliens' landing site.

finally leaves his family to search for the mountain.

The humans' communication with the aliens is expressed through musical notes played on a computer. John Williams, continuing his collaboration with Steven, composed an original musical score for the film. It included the now-famous five-note motif, a communicating theme between the mother ship and the scientists.

"I read the script and I was floored by it," said Steven's sister Sue. "There was so much of our childhood in that film—scenes of the children fighting and the parents fighting. When I saw it I burst out into tears. It was so much that I repressed of my parents fighting before the divorce."

Steven included many personal details in the movie. "My birthday was in there," said Sue. "When Richard Dreyfuss was being led on board the ship and the scientists are saying, 'What's your blood type? What's your birthday?' He said, 'December fourth.' He

---

"There was so much of our childhood in that film."
—Sue Spielberg

---

writes these little touches in of the family and I love watching for those little moments."

While writing the movie, Steven was inspired by the song "When You Wish Upon a Star" from Walt Disney's *Pinocchio*. Jiminy Cricket (voice of Cliff Edwards) sings the song in the Disney movie. "I pretty much hung my story on the mood the song created," said Steven, "the way it affected me emotionally."

Jiminy Cricket sings "When You Wish Upon a Star."

Steven invited his sisters to visit him during filming. "I was on location with *Close Encounters* for several weeks in Alabama and he had a room for us in his house. Nancy and I went and spent the summer with him in 1976," recalled Sue. "I so enjoy watching him film. I love watching him work with people. We were single and he was very protective of his sisters. On the set there are a lot of guys who make the moves on the girls."

While working on *Close Encounters* Steven himself became romantically involved with actress Amy Irving. He had met her when she auditioned for the role of Dreyfuss's wife. But at age twenty-two she was too young for the part. Months later Steven met Amy again at a dinner party and they began dating.

Soon they were living together with Steven's cocker spaniel and a pet parrot in a big new house in Beverly Hills.

"I don't want to be known as Steven's girlfriend," she told reporters. So for the next four years while they were a couple, they never worked together.

Close Encounters opened in November 1977 and received great reviews. Frank Rich in *Time* magazine wrote, "*Close Encounters* offers proof, if any were needed, that Spielberg's reputation is no accident. His new movie is richer than *Jaws*, and it reaches the viewer at a far more profound level than *Star Wars*." Although the movie was a critical and box office hit, Steven filmed new scenes two years later and re-edited the entire film to produce a Special Edition.

Steven received his first Oscar nomination as director of *Close Encounters*, but at the Academy Award presentations, he lost out to Woody Allen, director of *Annie Hall*. However, *Close Encounters* won two Oscars, one for Cinematography and one for Sound Effects Editing. Steven was very disappointed at not winning. He longed for the recognition of his peers. "Of course, it means a lot, winning anything, being recognized for your work—anyone who denies that isn't speaking from the heart," he said. "An Oscar would be wonderful, but for me, not the last goal.

"I hope, in the movie life, there is no last goal. That you make movies until your teeth fall out and you've retired to the motion picture home in the country."

From *Raiders of the Lost Ark* to *E.T.*

As a boy growing up in Phoenix, Steven loved going to the Kiva movie theater. "I was in the movies all day long, every Saturday," he recalled. For fifty cents' admission Steven and the other kids saw a program that included two feature-length movies, ten cartoons, *Our Gang* shorts, and installments of exciting serials filmed in the 1930s and '40s. "I saw *Tailspin Tommy* and *Masked Marvel* and *Commando Cody* and *Spy Smasher*—serials like that," said Steven. These serials left a lasting impression and later inspired his movie *Raiders of the Lost Ark*.

The idea for *Raiders* came about when Steven went on a vacation to Hawaii in May 1977 with his friend George Lucas. Lucas had just finished *Star Wars*, and Steven was taking a break from work on *Close Encounters*. They talked about doing a project together someday, perhaps an action-adventure movie like the serials they had both enjoyed as kids. "Movies set in exotic locales with a cliffhanger every second," said Lucas. "An adventure story of high intensity," said Steven. The result, two years later,

Just another day on the job for Commando Cody, *above*. Steven directing Harrison Ford in *Raiders of the Lost Ark, opposite page*.

was *Raiders of the Lost Ark*, produced by Paramount.

Although Steven didn't write the script, he and Lucas dreamed up many of the ideas, such as the opening sequence in which Indiana Jones ("Indy") runs for his life as he is chased by a gigantic boulder.

"An adventure story of high intensity."

Steven directing.

The film was set in 1936, reminiscent of the old serials.

But when Steven watched some of his old favorites, including *Don Winslow of the Navy,* he was stunned at how boring they were. Then he thought, "Holy smokes, if I got this excited about this stuff, it's going to be easy for me to get kids excited about the same thing, only better."

Steven spent months planning the action scenes

Steven, about 1980, *above.* E.T. with Steven, *opposite page.*

in collaboration with four artists who made hundreds of storyboards. In 1980 the cast and crew traveled to Tunisia, in North Africa, to begin shooting.

Karen Allen played the female lead, Marion Ravenwood. "In *Raiders* I dropped snakes on Karen Allen's head because I didn't think she was screaming for real, "said Steven. (He may have remembered playing the same trick, with a rubber snake, on the housekeeper back in Phoenix.)

Steven had considered casting Amy Irving as Marion Ravenwood. But around that time he and Amy split up. "Having come from a relationship with a very public man," says Amy, "I needed to go and find out what my life on my own was about." The breakup hurt Steven, but, he said, "I avoided all the grown-up pains by being too busy making movies."

Raiders starred Harrison Ford as Indy, and Ford's girlfriend, screenwriter Melissa Mathison, visited him on location. Filming took sixteen weeks, with London as the home base. Steven worked hard directing the movie. Lucas was on hand part of the time. When he and Steven disagreed about how a scene should be played, Lucas would say, '"Well, it's your movie. If the audience doesn't like it, they're going to blame you." Spielberg would answer, "Okay, but I'm going to tell them that *you* made me do it."

Steven finished ahead of schedule and stayed within the budget. Yet he felt depressed about the film. "Action is wonderful," he said later, "but while I was doing *Raiders* I felt I was losing touch with the reason I became a moviemaker—to make stories about people and relationships.

"I remember saying to myself, 'What I really need is a friend I can talk to—somebody who can give me *all* the answers.' I began concocting this imaginary creature, partially from the guys who stepped out of

"What if he needed me as much as I needed him?"

"I remember saying to myself, 'What I really need is a friend I can talk to—somebody who can give me *all* the answers.'"

the mother ship for ninety seconds in *Close Encounters* and then went back in, never to be seen again. Then I thought, 'What if I were ten years old again—where I've sort of been for thirty-four years anyway—and what if he needed me as much as I needed him? Wouldn't that be a great love story?'"

Steven told his idea to screenwriter Mathison. "He said he wanted to make a children's film about a person from outer space who gets stranded on Earth," she recalls. "We decided at the beginning that he should be benevolent and frightened and not some vicious monster." Mathison agreed to write the script and started work in October 1980, back in Los Angeles. Meanwhile, Steven, who had also returned to Los Angeles and was editing *Raiders*, sold his idea for *E.T.* to Universal. *Raiders* opened in 1981 and turned out to be another hit. Steven received his second Oscar nomination for best director, but he didn't win.

However, he was already working on *E.T.*, which he considered his most personal film.

"I wanted to tell the story of a lonely boy in a relationship with siblings, and I also wanted to tell

Drew Barrymore as Gertie in *E.T.*

the story of the divorce of my parents. Elliott's not me," he said in an interview, "but yes, he's the closest thing to my experience in life, growing up in suburbia.

"The house in *E.T.* is very much like the house I was raised in," said Steven. "That's my bedroom!"

Child actors headed the cast—eleven-year-old Henry Thomas as Elliott, Robert MacNaughton as Michael, and six-year-old Drew Barrymore as their sister, Gertie. Steven based the character of Gertie on his own sister Sue. "He told me that Gertie in *E.T.* was me between the ages of four and eight," recalls Sue. "He directed her [Drew Barrymore] and would tell her stories about me. He wanted her to have a little edge to her because I was a feisty little kid."

For this movie Steven did not use storyboards. "I decided that storyboards might smother the spontaneous reaction that young children might have to a sequence," he said. "So I purposely didn't do any storyboards and just came onto the set and winged it every day and made the movie as close to my own sensibilities and instincts as I possibly could."

Steven directing Henry Thomas, *above*. Elliott and E.T., *opposite page*.

In a videotaped interview eighteen years later, Drew and Henry recalled what it was like working with Steven.

"When I had to cry," said Drew, "he was amazing. He had this special way of talking to you and his voice would change and it made you cry. There was something so gentle about it."

And Henry said, "On the important scenes Steven would come up and I would have a ten-minute pep talk before we began." Every day during lunchtime Steven and Henry played video games together. "I felt the best way to work with Henry in *E.T.* was not to be his director, but his buddy," said Steven. He continued his friendship with the children he worked with and sent great holiday gifts.

"He always wanted to have fun," said Drew. "He encouraged it. On Halloween we were to dress up. Steven was a woman and he directed all day in the woman's costume. He looked great!"

Steven was filmed in his getup—skirt, blouse, hat, gloves, earrings, and pearls. "This is Halloween, folks," said Steven on camera. "I don't dress this way *all* the time."

E.T. was about Steven's childhood, and his childhood dreams. "It was very important to me that adults not be part of this children's world," said Steven, "that they have no identity until it's crucial to the story." He borrowed a device from cartoons made in the 1940s featuring cats and dogs as the main characters. "You'd never see the adults," said Steven. "You'd only see their legs." Similarly, in the opening scenes of *E.T.,* Steven showed only the legs of adult men—the bad guys who are pursuing E.T. Dee Wallace, playing the part of the children's mother, a sympathetic character, is unable to see or

recognize E.T. until close to the end, even when the creature is in plain sight.

Carlo Rambaldi, who had designed an alien puppet for *Close Encounters,* constructed E.T. Rambaldi wanted to make a single live action puppet, but soon found that he needed three separate E.T.s: one that could walk by itself, an electronic one for close shots of facial expressions, and an E.T. suit worn by small actors. "E.T. has [poet] Carl Sandburg's eyes," said Steven. A special feature of E.T. was a fingertip that lit up to heal, and to express love.

E.T. appeared believable and lovable because of the skillful work of Allen Daviau, director of photography. Daviau had filmed *Slipstream* and *Amblin',* and now Steven called on him again. "*E.T.* was my first major movie," said Daviau. "I remember when I read the script I said to Steven, 'It's got to be so real. The whole world around has to be absolutely realistic, so that the magic that happens isn't hokey.'"

Daviau and Steven began by discussing lighting. "Steven had a very good concept about that," said Daviau. 'We don't want to see E.T. We can't see him. Well, we've got to see him a little bit, but just a little bit.' The whole beginning of the thing was not to see him too well.

"I would go out to Carlo Rambaldi's place with a camera and I'd shoot a test of some new development in E.T., how Carlo was doing the mouth. And Steven would really react terribly if E.T. was in light, in full light. We had the idea by the time we got to the point of being serious, that when we saw E.T. we would just glimpse him moving through light, or he would be in a lowered light situation.

"Throughout the whole filming of *E.T.* it was always a question of, Where is he? Where is E.T.

going to be? Because where E.T. was located in a shot dictated how the lighting had to be set."

Music contributed greatly to the emotional pull of the film. Once again, John Williams composed the score. A melody played on a harp quietly introduces E.T. when he first meets Elliott in the sequence called "The Beginning of a Friendship." The same theme is heard again when Elliott declares, "I'm keeping him!" And at the end the exhilarating music soars as Elliott takes off on his bicycle with E.T. in the basket and flies silhouetted against the moon.

Steven said, "I've always felt that John Williams was my musical rewrite artist. He comes in, sees my movie, rewrites the whole thing musically, and makes it much better than I did. He can take a moment and just uplift it."

The movie premiered at the Cannes Film Festival in France in May 1982. Kathleen Kennedy, producer of *E.T.*, described the event as "magical."

Near the end of the movie, when E.T.'s finger lit up on the screen to show that he was alive, "lighters started to light and matches started to be struck, so there was this starlight effect in the theater," she remembered. "You couldn't even hear the end of the movie because people were on their feet stomping and yelling. And this huge searchlight started to sweep the top balcony to find us, and Steven stood up. It was one of the most amazing experiences."

In June there was a special screening of *E.T.* at the White House for President Ronald Reagan and his wife, Nancy.

"Nancy was crying toward the end, and the president looked like a ten-year-old kid," Steven remembered.

E.T. broke all box-office records and brought Steven worldwide fame. His mother appeared on television on the *Tonight Show* and told host Johnny Carson stories about Steven's childhood. In December Steven was presented to Queen Elizabeth II at a royal benefit showing of *E.T.* in London.

But not everyone liked the movie. Journalist George F. Will wrote a *Newsweek* column entitled "Well, *I* Don't Love You, E.T." And film critic Vincent Canby of the *New York Times* wrote that the film "freely recycles elements from all sorts of earlier children's works, including *Peter Pan* and *The Wizard of Oz*."

Despite the criticisms, *E.T.* touched audiences everywhere. The movie received nine Oscar nomina-

> ## "I thought *E.T.* was the more exciting, wonderful, innovative piece of film."
> —*Richard Attenborough*

tions and won for Best Music, Sound, Sound Effects, and Special Effects. Steven was nominated as Best Director for the third time but lost to Richard Attenborough for *Gandhi*. Attenborough, a friend of Steven's, said, "I thought *E.T.* was the more exciting, wonderful, innovative piece of film."

Steven appreciated praise from a director he greatly admired. However, he said, "If the Academy decides to give me an Oscar someday, I'll be glad to accept it. But I don't think I'll get it for a film that I really care about. *E.T.* is my favorite movie."

The Color Purple and *Empire of the Sun*

The pleasure of working with child actors on *E.T.* gave Steven a desire to have his own family. He said he had a "deep yearning now to become a father." But the demands of his career gave him little time for a social life. As soon as he finished one project, he was on to the next. "I didn't ever take the time to revel in the glory of a successful or money-making film," he said in an interview. "I haven't done that because I put my moviemaking ahead of some of the results. I thought that if I stopped I would never get started again, that I would lose the momentum."

After *E.T.* he collaborated again with George Lucas on *Indiana Jones and the Temple of Doom*, a prequel that told the story of what happened before *Raiders of the Lost Ark*. It featured a new young actress, Kate Capshaw, who was later to become very important in Steven's life.

In *The Temple of Doom* Steven stepped up the pace of action-adventure. He and Lucas created villains who deal in black magic, torture, and slavery—"truly evil villains," said Steven. As a result, he was criticized for making a film that was too violent. One scene, showing a man having his heart plucked out as a human sacrifice, especially upset viewers and critics.

"There are parts of this film that are too intense for younger children, but this is a fantasy adventure," Steven said in his own defense. "It is the kind of violence that does not really happen, will not really happen." Yet he later said, "*Indy Two* will not go down in my pantheon as one of my prouder moments."

When Steven flew to India to scout locations for *Temple of Doom*, Amy Irving surprised him by meeting him at the airport. She was in India working on a TV miniseries. Steven and Amy resumed their relationship. "We fell in love again," he said. In 1984, much to Steven's delight, Amy became pregnant.

That year marked another milestone—Steven formed Amblin Entertainment with Kathleen Kennedy and Frank Marshall, producers of some of his movies. The visual image of Elliott and E.T. silhouetted against the moon became the company's logo.

Amblin's headquarters were located on the back lot of Universal. The pueblo-style compound contained a screening room (with a popcorn and candy counter), cutting rooms, video arcade, kitchen staffed by a professional chef, gym, and wishing well with a miniature *Jaws* shark. Steven decorated the place in a southwestern style that reminded him of Phoenix and hung movie posters and paintings by Norman Rockwell on the walls.

Rockwell's art particularly appealed to Steven. One of the first Rockwell paintings that Steven bought for his own collection was *Spirit of America, 1929,* a portrait of a Boy Scout. "I first came across Rockwell when I was a Boy Scout," said Steven in an interview for *Berkshire* magazine. "Our troop in Scottsdale, Arizona, had a Rockwell poster [*Spirit of America*] that celebrated scouting, which we saw every Friday night at assembly. I was twelve."

Since childhood Steven had had a terrible fear of heights, so Amblin's building was only two stories high. He also had another phobia: "He's terrified of elevators," says his sister Anne. "He wrote a poem when he was in high school before I ever knew he had a fear of elevators. He must have been grappling

with it himself." Steven was fourteen or fifteen when he wrote "Elevator." It began:

Seven, six, five,
Will I arrive at four?
Or will I crumple? Will I bounce?
Oh, there's the second floor.

So there are no elevators at Amblin.

Fears and terrors continued to influence Steven. At Amblin he encouraged and developed the ideas of other young filmmakers and produced *Gremlins*, *The Goonies*, and a comedy, *Back to the Future*. Then, in 1984, his partner, Kathleen Kennedy, gave him a book and said, "Here's something you might enjoy reading."

It was *The Color Purple* by Alice Walker. The novel tells of a black woman named Celie who is abused by her father, then her husband, but courageously endures her suffering and triumphs in the end. "I started reading it and I couldn't stop," said Steven. "I came away from it very much in love with Celie."

Although Kennedy had not thought of the book as a potential film project, Steven did. He recalled discussing it with composer Quincy Jones, one of the film's producers. Steven said to Quincy, "I don't know that I'm the filmmaker for this. Don't you want to find a black director or a woman?" And Quincy asked, "You didn't have to come from Mars to do *E.T.*, did you?" He said, "This movie should be directed by the person who loves it most," and Steven said, "I loved it more than anyone else."

Steven met Alice Walker, and she approved of him as director of the film. "My color was never an issue after she selected me as the right guy for the

"*The Color Purple* is the biggest challenge of my career."

picture," said Steven. "The issue was not the color of my skin, but whether I'd make a good movie out of the book."

Whoopi Goldberg, until that time best known as a stand-up comic, was chosen to play the part of Celie, and Oprah Winfrey, the talk-show host, was cast as Celie's friend Sofia. Neither Whoopi nor Oprah had ever appeared in a movie before. When they started filming in June 1985, Alice Walker often visited the set, giving advice and adding lines when needed. "The Color Purple is the biggest challenge of my career," said Steven in an interview during filming.

Allen Daviau, who had worked with him on E.T., was director of photography. "The winter scenes, people walking around out in the snow, were all done in August in North Carolina," says Daviau. The movie opens with a close-up of purple wildflowers. Then the camera pulls back to show two girls in the distance happily clapping hands and dancing through the field. "It was Steven's vision of how it was going to open, tracking the girls through the flowers," says Daviau. "The flowers were planted exclusively for that shot." But there was a glitch.

The head greensman planted seeds from a packet showing a purple blossom. "When the flowers bloomed," says Daviau, "which is while we were shooting the movie, they came up pink. So we corrected it in the lab as much as we could."

The first weeks of filming took place on the lot at Universal in Los Angeles. Just a few days after they started production, they were doing a scene in which Celie gives birth. "The assistant director broke in to tell me that Amy was on the phone," recalled Steven. She had gone into labor. Amy said to Steven, "Okay, come home to deliver *my* baby now."

Max Samuel Spielberg was born on June 13, 1985,

and Steven described his son as "my biggest and best production of the year." The baby's cries heard in *The Color Purple* were actually those of Max, recorded by Steven at home while the baby was taking a bath. Five months later, in November, Steven and Amy were married.

The Color Purple opened in movie theaters on Steven's thirty-ninth birthday on December 18, 1985. The movie received eleven Oscar nominations, including one for Daviau as cinematographer, but none for Steven as director. When the Academy Awards were presented at the ceremony in March, *The Color Purple* did not receive a single Oscar. Many people felt that Steven and the movie itself had been snubbed. However, Steven did get his first Directors Guild of America Award.

If Steven was disappointed, he didn't let his feelings slow him down. His next film, *Empire of the Sun*, was also based on a book, an autobiographical novel by J. G. Ballard about his experiences as a British boy separated from his parents in Japanese-occupied Shanghai during World War II. "From the moment I read the novel," said Steven, "I wanted to do it. I was attracted to the main character being a child."

The boy in the novel, Jim Graham, ages from eleven to fifteen as he struggles to survive in a Japanese prison camp without his parents. More than four thousand young actors auditioned for the part. Then Amy recommended thirteen-year-old Christian Bale, who had worked with her in a television feature, and he was chosen.

Allen Daviau was director of photography once again. Filming took place in China and England. This was the adult Steven's first movie about World War II, and in it he explored themes that were important to him—a child's separation from his mother and father,

Nettie (Akosua Busia) and young Celie (Desreta Jackson) play hand games in the field of purple flowers, *opposite page, top.* Anne and Sue Spielberg holding hands in their yard, *bottom.*

Steven with one of his planes.

the painful process of growing up, and a fascination with airplanes.

"As a child I used to build model planes," recalled Steven, "and I was attached to flying the way Jim is." Jim greatly admires fliers, even enemy kamikaze pilots he sees from a distance when he is imprisoned in the Japanese camp. "I consciously like flying and have flying in all of my films," Steven said. "But I'm afraid to fly in real life, so there's an interesting conflict here."

Tom Stoppard wrote the screenplay, but Steven, a visual storyteller, added many personal touches. Norman Rockwell, Steven's favorite artist, again provided inspiration. The director used a painting, *Freedom from Fear, 1943*, depicting a mother and father tucking in their son at bedtime, as a reference for one of the early scenes showing Jim safely at home. During the movie Jim carries a copy of the painting, torn from a magazine, wherever he goes.

Novelist Ballard was enormously pleased with the film. *Empire of the Sun* received five nominations for Oscars, including one for Allen Daviau as Best Cinematographer. "I feel very sorry that I get nomi-

nations and Steven doesn't," says Daviau. The film won no awards. Yet it helped Steven make a transition to what he called "grown-up stories."

Filming *Empire of the Sun* kept him away from home for long periods of time. Steven and Amy flew back and forth across the ocean to visit each other and be with their son. But juggling two separate careers added problems to their marriage, and in 1989 they divorced. Later in a televised interview, Steven said that the two worst times in his life were the divorce of his parents and his divorce from Amy.

Kate Capshaw, the actress who had played the female lead in *Indiana Jones and the Temple of Doom*, came back into Steven's life, and soon they were a couple. Kate had a daughter, Jessica, from a previous marriage, and a foster child, Theo, whom she and Spielberg later adopted. In 1990 Kate and Steven had a baby of their own, a daughter, Sasha. Kate converted to Judaism, and in 1991 she and Steven were married.

Together they planned to focus on their large family. In an interview for the *New York Times* Steven said, "I want to stop having kids on the screen and have them in real life."

Steven and Kate Capshaw, *right*. A scene from *Empire of the Sun, opposite page,* and *Freedom from Fear, 1943,* the Norman Rockwell painting that provided inspiration.

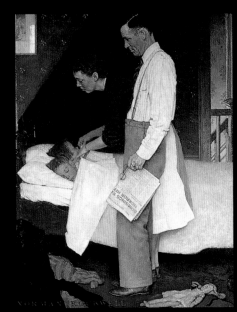

"From the moment I read the novel, I wanted to do it. I was attracted to the main character being a child."

Jurassic Park

"I've been interested in dinosaurs since I was a child," said Steven. "I remember always collecting dinosaur models and being interested in the fantastic *size* of these creatures.

"There's a quote from a Harvard psychologist who was asked why kids love dinosaurs so much. He said, 'That's easy. They're big, they're fierce . . . and they're dead.'"

As a boy Steven went on field trips to the site where the Hadrosaurus foulkii had been discovered—right in Haddonfield, N.J., where he lived. The fossil was the first nearly complete dinosaur skeleton found in modern history.

So years later, in 1989, when author Michael Crichton told Steven about a new book he had written called *Jurassic Park*, a novel about dinosaurs, Steven asked to read it immediately. The next day he told Crichton that he wanted to buy the film rights. By May 1990, after a bidding war with competing studios, Crichton chose Steven to produce and direct the movie. "I knew it was going to be a very difficult picture to make," said Crichton. "Steven is arguably the most experienced and most successful director of these kinds of movies."

Steven framing an image, *left*. Steven with triceratops, *below*. Tim (Joseph Mazzello), Dr. Ellie Sattler (Laura Dern), Dr. Alan Grant (Sam Neill), and Lex (Ariana Richards) try to keep a safe distance from an approaching dinosaur, *opposite page*.

"I was really just trying to make a good sequel to *Jaws*. On land."

"What's going to be scariest is when you hear this breathing and the nose comes in the window . . . "

"With *Jurassic* I was really just trying to make a good sequel to *Jaws*. On land," said Steven.

"*Jurassic Park* is a cross between a zoo and a theme park," Steven said. "It's about the idea that man has been able to bring dinosaurs back to earth millions and millions of years later, and what happens when we come together."

Jurassic Park tells of billionaire John Hammond, portrayed by Lord Richard Attenborough, who finds a dinosaur-biting insect preserved in amber. Hammond takes DNA from dinosaur blood and clones various dinosaurs—Tyrannosaurus rex, triceratops, and velociraptors—and puts them in a theme park. "Our attraction will drive kids out of their minds," he says gleefully at the beginning of the movie.

But things get out of control when the dinosaurs run wild and go after Hammond and his grandchildren—Tim, played by nine-year-old Joseph Mazzello, and Lex, played by twelve-year-old Ariana Richards.

Ariana had been appearing in movies since she was eight. Steven especially liked her performance in *Disaster in Time*, and he invited her to try out for the part of Lex. "He wanted me to come in and audition screaming," recalls Ariana. "I went in and auditioned and screamed my little heart out. Then we just chatted for a while, talked about the movie, about me and my interests—stuff like that. And after a while he said, 'So, are you busy in August?' and I said, 'No, no, why?' And that was it." Ariana had the part.

Despite the violence of the dinosaurs, Steven wanted to present them as animals rather than as monsters, and he discussed their individual traits with Crichton. He outlined their "physical appearances, their hopes and fears, their quirks," recalled Crichton.

Tim hides from velociraptors, *opposite page*. Storyboard from *Jurassic Park*, *right*.

Steven thought about how fast they would move and "talked about a Tyrannosaurus rex sprinting sixty miles an hour, chasing a car." Crichton said, "Steven, how are you going to *do* this?" Steven shrugged and said, "Effects are only as good as the audience's feeling for the characters."

Preproduction began in 1990 and took two years. Before there was even a script, Steven storyboarded scenes and drew some of the frames himself, carefully planning the action and special effects. He had

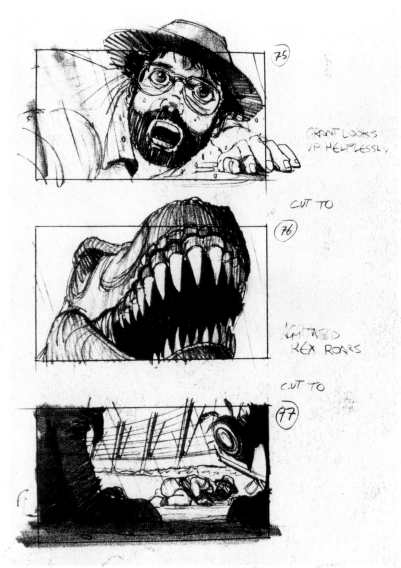

Making Dinosaurs

An artist makes drawings of dinosaurs as they might have looked.

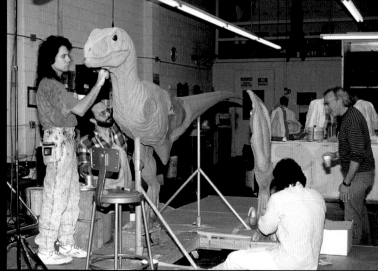

Stan Winston's design team creates sculptures to determine the look of each dinosaur character.

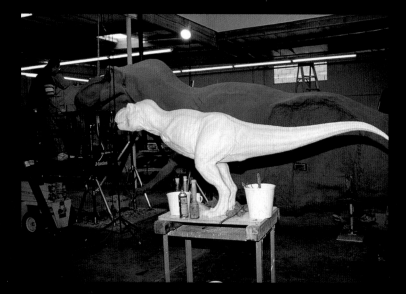

A dinosaur sculpture waits to be painted.

Artists paint a full-size model of Tyrannosaurus rex.

artists do big sketches for the many complicated scenes. Later, when filming began, they brought the sketches for a particular scene to the set and pasted them near the camera. Steven gathered cast and crew around the drawings to study them before shooting. This way everyone was in sync with what he wanted at the outset.

Designer Stan Winston was hired to build life-size dinosaurs. Winston and his staff of engineers and artists created a twenty-foot-tall Tyrannosaurus rex weighing 13,000 pounds that was operated by remote controls. For the velociraptors, they made a full-sized mechanical puppet and an animal suit that could be worn by an actor.

Steven helped plan details such as the dinosaurs' head movements and breathing. In the scene when Tyrannosaurus rex attacks Hammond's grandchildren in their stalled car, Steven said, "What's going to be scariest is when you hear this breathing and the nose comes in the window and you see the breathing against the glass."

"Steven did most of the roars off camera," recalls Ariana. Although she *looked* terrified, she was acting. "I just imagined myself in the situation with horrible monsters like that, and the dinosaurs were scary-looking enough to facilitate my getting into that state of mind.

"And he would sometimes say to me after doing one of those scenes, 'Oh, you looked so scared, Ariana! How do you get to this depth of fear? Were you scared by a clown or something when you were two [as Steven was himself]? Oh, wait, I don't want to know. Don't tell me.'"

Steven had miniature models made for scenes showing the dinosaurs stampeding. But he thought these models wouldn't look convincing, so he went to Industrial Light and Magic (ILM), a special-effects

Physical effects specialist Stan Winston (right) tells Lord Richard Attenborough how the dinosaur models work.

company owned by his friend George Lucas. The ILM team of technical and graphic artists created a computer-generated stampede and a Tyrannosaurus rex.

When the T. rex first appeared on the screen, said ILM's effects supervisor, Dennis Murren, "Everybody went absolutely crazy. It was like nothing anyone had ever seen before." Steven said the effects were "so authentic, I couldn't believe my eyes." He decided not to use the miniature models after all, and relied solely on the computer-generated images and Winston's full-size models.

Although the movie was set off the coast of Costa Rica, filming took place on the Hawaiian island of Kauai and began on August 24, 1992. On September 11, the last scheduled day of shooting on location, a hurricane struck Kauai. Steven and the cast and crew took cover in the ballroom of their hotel.

"If you're going to be stranded with anyone, be stranded with a movie crew," said producer Kathleen Kennedy. "We had generators for lights, and plenty of food and water. We were self-sustaining because we moved around on location all the time."

That day happened to be Ariana Richards's thirteenth birthday. "The storm knocked part of the roof in, but nobody was hurt," she recalled. "Steven kept all of us kids entertained. He told us ghost stories and played cards for the whole twelve hours that the hurricane was going over us. I was scared of those ghost stories for a long time, but I got fun out of being thrilled. It was fun to be scared. But I always think of that man in all black in the shadows that he told me about."

Ariana's mother, who always accompanied her on the set, says, "I think he scared us worse than the hurricane when he told us *his* hurricane story."

"It actually turned out to be a pretty good birthday," says Ariana.

Months later, she saw the movie for the first time at a private screening for the cast. "I was blown away," said Ariana. "Scenes where there hadn't been any dinosaurs before like that one where we're being stampeded in the field—it was just breathtaking! I actually would really get scared as I was watching it. I would get startled and I would jump in my seat even though I had been on the set."

Jurassic Park was released on June 10, 1993, and was a huge box-office hit. The film earned hundreds of millions of dollars worldwide, making it the most financially successful film up to that time. "There were premieres of it all over the world," says Ariana. "I had the opportunity to travel and do some PR [public relations] for *Jurassic Park*. I went to Paris, Tokyo, and a premiere in London, which Steven attended." When they were introduced to Princess Diana, Ariana gave her a bouquet of white roses. "I followed Steven's request that we curtsy and say,

Ariana Richards, Steven Spielberg, and Princess Diana.

'Good evening, Your Majesty,'" she recalls. "Steven and other members of the cast kept it pretty informal."

Steven's fans clamored for a sequel to *Jurassic Park*. "There was such an outpouring of demand from the public," he said. "Thousands and thousands of letters."

An elementary-school class near San Francisco wrote to Steven and the scriptwriter, David Koepp. One of the kids suggested adding a stegosaurus to the next movie and said, "Whatever you do, please don't have a long, boring part at the beginning that has nothing to do with the island."

Steven and Koepp listened to these suggestions and added an adult and baby stegosaurus to *The Lost World: Jurassic Park*. But Steven didn't begin the film until a few years later.

When he finished editing the first *Jurassic Park*, he was already at work on a very different movie, *Schindler's List*.

Schindler's List

"Everything I have done up till now has really been a preparation for *Schindler*," Steven Spielberg said in 1993. "I had to grow into that."

Steven first became interested in *Schindler's List,* a novel by Australian author Thomas Keneally, when it was published in 1982. The book was based on the true-life story of a Holocaust survivor. The survivor, Poldek Pfefferberg (known as Leopold Page after he moved to the United States) and his wife had escaped death at the hands of the Nazis because of the heroic efforts of Oskar Schindler. Schindler, an industrialist and member of the Czech Nazi Party during World War II, saved more than a thousand Jews from going to the death camp Auschwitz-Birkenau.

Although Schindler's motives were selfish at first, he ultimately spent his fortune doing a virtuous deed that won him the title of Righteous Gentile from Yad Vashem in Israel. Yad Vashem is a worldwide organization devoted to researching the Holocaust and remembering the six million Jews who perished.

"I had a hunger to make *Schindler's List* a few months after *E.T. The Extra-Terrestrial* opened," said Steven. "I wanted to document it for the public

Steven on the set of *Schindler's List.*

record." But it took him ten years before he began the project. "I was afraid that when I bought the book I wasn't emotionally ready to take a chance with the Holocaust," he said. "And I waited until I thought I could."

"Please, when are you starting?" Leopold Page asked Steven when they met in 1983.

"Ten years from now," Steven answered.

Steven's mother also hoped he would make the movie. "We of the family kept saying to Steve over the many years, 'When are you going to do *Schindler's List*?'

He would just shut us all up with, 'I'm not ready.'"

"When he's ready to do something, he'll do it. And if he's not ready, there's nothing on this earth that can make him," says his sister Anne.

"And when he was ready, boy, he knew it," says Steven's mother, Leah Adler.

"[The story] was about a Nazi saving Jews," said Steven. "What would drive a man like this to suddenly take everything he had earned and put it all in the service of saving these lives? I didn't go to work on it right away because I didn't know *how* to do it."

Leopold Page, *left,* and Steven.

Steven may have been influenced by his wife's conversion to Judaism and by the emphasis on religious practices and beliefs in their household. By 1993 he felt prepared to face his own identity as a Jew. He remembered the anti-Semitism he had experienced as a teenager in high school and wanted to explore those painful feelings. And he was worried about surveys that showed that sixty percent of recent American high-school graduates had never even heard of the Holocaust.

From the start, Steven wanted to give *Schindler's List* the quality of a documentary. Before filming, he viewed documentaries about the Holocaust such as Claude Lanzmann's *Shoah*. Steven decided to make his film almost entirely in black and white so that it would look like newsreel footage shot in the forties. Janus Kaminski, director of photography, used a hand-held camera for much of the film. There was no crane, dolly, or zoom lens—all common movie-making tools used as a matter of course since the 1950s. "We want people to see this film in fifteen years and not have a sense of when it was made," said Kaminski.

Steven insisted on filming in actual locations—

Jerry Molen and Steven.

the streets of Krakow, Poland, in the old Jewish ghetto; Schindler's factory and apartment building; and Auschwitz. However, the World Jewish Congress refused to let Steven film inside the camp; the group feared he would make a Hollywood version of the Holocaust. He solved the problem by constructing a replica of the camp right next to Auschwitz.

Producer Jerry Molen went to Poland with Steven to scout locations. Back in Los Angeles he met Branko Lustig, a Croatian who had done many films in Poland. As a child Branko had been imprisoned at Auschwitz and had lost all of his family, except for his mother, in the concentration camps. "Branko

Branko Lustig, Jerry Molen, and Steven.

rolled up his sleeve and showed his number that had been tattooed in Auschwitz," recalled Jerry. "I knew this was the man [to work on the film] and said, 'You have to meet Steven.'" They met, and Branko became co-producer of *Schindler's List*.

Filming began on March 1, 1993, in bitterly cold weather. Steven needed to shoot in the snow for authenticity. When actor Liam Neeson, portraying Schindler, complained about the freezing tempera-

Steven, Leopold Page, and Liam Neeson.

actress Adi Nitzan, who portrayed Page's wife, said, "I remember my first day on the set, going to lunch and seeing six Nazis in uniform, eating, talking German. I couldn't accept them, sitting there and eating. They looked so beautiful and elegantly dressed. I looked down at my torn and tattered dress and wanted to cry."

Steven felt disturbed and angry as he directed his cast of thousands in a reenactment of horrific events

Steven on location.

tures, Branko showed him his tattoo, reminding him that the malnourished Jews dressed in rags had suffered far greater hardships in the same cold weather.

"I believe a divine hand was sitting on Steven's shoulder throughout the filming process," said Jerry Molen. "When we needed snow, it snowed. If we didn't need snow, it stopped."

To make *Schindler's List*, Steven had to coordinate and direct a huge number of people. The film had 126 speaking parts, 3,000 extras, 210 crew members, and 148 sets in thirty-five locations. "Directing a movie is like running an army," says Marvin Levy, spokesperson for Steven Spielberg. "Steven is commander-in-chief."

For crowd scenes, extras had to report at 5 A.M. for their costumes. Costume people gave them their clothes and made sure that they wore the same things every day. For Steven to tell the extras what he wanted them to do, translators were hired to interpret his directions from English into various languages. A Yugoslav catering firm set up a buffet in a tent to feed the actors and technicians. Israeli

"In so many
American
schools, the
Holocaust
really is a
footnote in
the history
books."

"My kids saw me cry for the first time. I would

that had really happened. "I feel like more of a journalist than a director on this movie," he said. "I feel like I'm reporting more than creating. I re-created these events, and then I experienced them as any witness or victim would have. It wasn't like a movie."

What made the project bearable for him was the presence of his family. Kate and their five children—Max, Jessica, Theo, Sasha, and Sawyer, a son born in 1992—stayed in Poland with him during the three months of filming. "We wanted the kids to be there," said Steven. "We wanted the kids to know about this.

"My kids saw me cry for the first time. I would come home and weep."

Steven invited his mother and her husband to visit him on location. "I went to Poland when he was filming," recalls Leah Adler. "He wanted me to come

Bernie and Leah Adler with Steven on location.

watch him do it. And my husband was so ill at that time. I said, 'Steve, it's impossible.' He said, 'I'll send your doctors with you.' And he did. We all went with a medical team."

One scene in particular moved Leah. In that scene Jewish mothers run screaming after trucks that take away their unsuspecting children to Auschwitz and certain death. When that moment appears in the film, a melancholy folk song is heard. It is called *"Oifen Pripetchik"* and is sung in Yiddish by a children's choir. It is an alphabet song used to teach children their letters. *Oifen pripetchik* means "the flames are burning in the fireplace."

"My grandmother used to sing that song to us when we were kids," remembers Anne.

John Williams composed the score for *Schindler's List*. "The first thing I do is watch

Steven and his sisters with Grandma Becky, who sang "Oifen Pripetchik" to them.

the film with Steven after it's completed," said Williams. "I would rather not know what's coming

---

"I feel like more of a journalist than a director on this movie."

---

and get my first impression of the film as though I were the audience. Afterward, we discuss the score, where there should be music. We exchange ideas."

Williams saw *Schindler's List* at Steven's house in East Hampton, New York, and found it "staggering, hugely impressive. It was a dramatic re-creation of history."

Williams said to Steven, "You need a better composer than I am."

"I know," said Steven. "But they're all dead."

John Williams at work.

Williams wrote the score at the piano. "Piano has been my tool all my life," he said. "I do my work there." Later, on the soundtrack recording, he played a piano solo of the slow, haunting theme.

Steven was thrilled with the music, and he had an idea. "I think this would be fabulous on the violin," he said.

Williams called world-famous concert violinist Itzhak Perlman, played the themes for Perlman over the phone, and convinced him to perform the music for the soundtrack recording.

Steven arranged a private screening of the movie for his mother before it was released to the public. "I saw it in an empty theater," Leah says, "just my husband and I. They showed it and when I came out Steve's secretary was standing in the door with Steve on the phone. He wanted an impression. I was totally mute. I thought I would never speak again."

Anne saw *Schindler's List* at the Simon Wiesenthal Center/Museum of Tolerance in Los Angeles. "It was the quietest [screening], except for actual sobbing out loud. Sobbing, not crying, sobbing," she remem-

bers. "At the end of that film I've never seen people more dazed and quiet, and needing to be really by themselves as they walked out. They all started moving toward their own cars. There wasn't this hanging around afterward, let's talk about this movie. Nobody could talk."

"*Schindler's* hit me like a ton of bricks," says Steven's sister Nancy. "Seeing it was probably one of my proudest moments."

In March 1994, at the Academy Award ceremonies, the Spielberg family sat beaming and cheering as *Schindler's List* won an Oscar for Best Picture. The Academy gave the movie six more awards, including one to John Williams for Best Original Score, and another to Janus Kaminski for Best Cinematography. Finally, Steven won his Oscar as

"Staggering, hugely impressive. It was a dramatic re-creation of history."—*John Williams*

Best Director. In his acceptance speech he thanked "the six million who can't be watching this among the one billion watching this telecast tonight. In so many American schools, the Holocaust really is a footnote in the history books."

"Every day was filled with emotion," recalls Molen, thinking about the making of the movie. "Atrocities of the past. As Steven said so eloquently, 'I'm standing right here where fifty years ago people were loaded on trucks. If it were not for a different time . . .'" There were tears in everyone's eyes.

The Shoah Foundation

"I have a story to tell. Will you hear my story?" said many Holocaust survivors to Steven during the filming of *Schindler's List* and after its release. "At first I thought, 'Are you saying you want me to make a movie out of your story?'" Steven said. "But what they were really saying was, 'Will you take my testimony? Can I, before I die, tell somebody—tell you, with a camera—what happened to me, so my children will know, so my friends will finally know, and so I can leave something of myself behind so the world will know?'

"Enough people came to me," recalled Steven, "that I realized that this really was the reason I made *Schindler's List* . . . to do this project."

In September 1994, he founded the Survivors of the Shoah Visual History Foundation with his earnings from the movie. *"Shoah"* is the Hebrew name for the

Steven with Bert Strauss, a survivor featured on the educational CD-ROM, and a student at Whitney Young High School in Chicago.

"I have a story to tell. Will you hear my story?"

Holocaust. Steven said, "I felt that a much more important contribution to remembering the Shoah would be to create an audio-visual archive of firsthand testimonies."

The process of making *Schindler's List* had profoundly affected Steven. "He went through life changes," says his sister Anne. "Religious changes. I've never seen anybody change so much.

"I was startled by this turnaround with Steve's life. The movie, how he viewed the world, his sense of religion, his sense of people, his sense of the whole Holocaust."

Steven especially wanted to educate young people and help them "wake up to the fact that we are all part of history." His goals in forming the Shoah Foundation were to record firsthand accounts of the Holocaust from those who had survived, and to develop a multimedia archive.

"The majority of Holocaust survivors are in their seventies and eighties," said Steven. "The window for capturing their testimonies is closing fast. This archive will preserve history as told by the people who lived it and lived through it."

The foundation's goals have always been to also record testimony from non-Jewish survivors—Gypsies, Jehovah's Witnesses, homosexuals, and other minorities the Nazis regarded as "subhuman."

Steven put together a team of people to work on the project. Jerry Molen and Branko Lustig, the producers of *Schindler's List,* were on the founding advisory committee. Other members of the team included child survivors such as Branko. Another survivor, Director for Foundation Relations Daisy Miller, says, "We wanted to allow the survivors to tell their stories in their own words." Volunteers were trained in how to conduct interviews. "I generally ask people to give me a picture of what life was like before the war, their family life, then they start talking about their wartime experience. Once the floodgates open, memories return."

Mel Mermelstein, the only member of his family to survive the concentration camps, recalled his father's dying wish. "His last words were that if I ever did get out, I was to tell the world," says Mel.

An outreach program created awareness of the foundation. Survivors called a toll-free line to set up appointments or sent letters with their request.

Thousands of volunteer interviewers were trained all over the world and conducted interviews in fifty-seven countries from Argentina to the Ukraine, videotaping survivors in their own homes, where they would feel more comfortable.

The interviewers began by asking their subjects to fill out a questionnaire, providing the names of their parents, brothers, and sisters, and the towns or cities where they had lived when the Nazis came to power. Then a videographer did the filming while an interviewer asked questions off camera. Often the testimonies ended on a positive note, with the survivors telling how they had rebuilt their lives after the war and showing pictures of their children and grandchildren, new generations. The average taping lasts two hours and fifteen minutes, but some take as long as eight hours. Every survivor receives a VHS copy of his or her interview. A master copy is preserved in an underground vault at the foundation's headquarters in Los Angeles. There the testimonies are still being cataloged and digitized into a computer format.

Information is cross-referenced to provide valuable facts—for instance, the names of towns that no longer exist, and the dates when they were destroyed. "We're re-creating lost pieces of history," said one of the volunteer interviewers.

Within six years, more than fifty thousand testimonies had been gathered throughout the world. Eventually all of these will be accessible via computer. "My whole dream," said Steven, "is to take as many

Video transfer department.

testimonies as is humanly possible and make their stories available for no fee for those who want it."

The Shoah Foundation, under Steven's direction, has also produced a CD-ROM for educational purposes. It is called *Survivors: Testimonies of the Holocaust*, and traces the experiences of four survivors—Bert, Paula,

Cataloging department at the Shoah Foundation.

Silvia, and Sol. By clicking an icon, the viewer can see and hear any one of these survivors tell about his or her prewar life, imprisonment, and ultimate liberation. "It is essential that we see their faces, hear their voices, and understand that the horrors of the Holocaust happened to people like us," says Steven in the opening.

"To learn history, you have to look in history's eye. Here we have the unique opportunity to have the participants and witnesses of an event look us in the eye and say, 'This happened to me.'"

The CD-ROM is narrated by Leonardo DiCaprio and Winona Ryder, who donated their time. It is available to students in schools across the country.

The Shoah Foundation has also produced three documentaries, including *The Last Days*. This 1998 Academy Award–winning film tells of the terrible hardships faced

"To learn history, you have to look in history's eye."

by Hungarian Holocaust survivors at the end of the war and even after liberation.

Hundreds of people volunteer their time and services at the Shoah Foundation. One of them is Steven's father. "I do whatever I can to help out," Arnold Spielberg says. "I worked a lot with the cataloging department. Now I'm working with the Internet people on a national writing project that will help teachers prepare a curriculum for teaching tolerance and social justice.

Steven said, "I've dedicated the rest of my life to being involved in taking testimony as long as there are survivors who want to volunteer it."

DreamWorks Presents
Saving Private Ryan

"Hey, Let's Put On a Show!" read the headline in a *Time* magazine article. The line came from an old musical, *Babes In Arms*, about teenage kids putting on a show together. The "kids" in the *Time* article, however, referred to Steven and his friends Jeffrey Katzenberg and David Geffen. On October 12, 1994, they announced the creation of their own film, TV, music, and interactive video company.

Each man brought a particular strength to the enterprise. Katzenberg had been the chairman of Walt Disney Studios and was responsible for hit animated films including *The Little Mermaid*, *Beauty and the Beast*, and *The Lion King*. Geffen had his own record company, Geffen Records, which made stars of the Eagles, Guns N' Roses, and Nirvana. He had also produced successful movies—*Beetlejuice* and *Interview with the Vampire*, among others. Steven, of course, was one of the top filmmakers in Hollywood.

At a press conference he said, "I want to create a place driven by ideas, and the people who have them." All three partners invested millions of their own money in the new company. Steven said they wanted to "be the owners of our own dreams." The press called them "The Dream Team," and the name stuck. Steven suggested changing it to DreamWorks, and they added the initials of their last names, resulting in "DreamWorks SKG." Their logo shows a little boy with a fishing pole off in the clouds sitting on the edge of a crescent moon.

"The logo was a Steven idea," says his spokesperson, Marvin Levy. "It represents trolling for ideas," or in other words, casting a line in hopes of hooking something. The partners wanted to give new young filmmakers the opportunity to fulfill their dreams.

At the age of forty-eight, Steven felt ready to take on the responsibility of heading a huge multimedia company with his partners. "Ten years ago this would have been inconceivable because I love

Setting out to save Private Ryan are Private Caparzo (Vin Diesel), Private Reiben (Edward Burns), Sergeant Horvath (Tom Sizemore), Private Jackson (Barry Pepper), and Corporal Upham (Jeremy Davies), with Private Mellish (Adam Goldberg) behind him, *opposite page*.

"I was looking for realism all the time."

"We were making a serious picture about war."

80

having bosses in my life . . . I needed them," he said. "But I grew up and began to foster children and have a large family. I felt I was ready to be the father of my own business. Or at least the co-father."

Steven's wife, Kate, worried that he would spend too much time at his combined jobs of directing movies, running the Shoah Foundation, and producing multimedia for DreamWorks. She knew that Katzenberg had a reputation for being a workaholic. So Kate told Katzenberg, "You can have him [Steven] after he takes the kids to school, but you'd better deliver him back here by five-thirty at night."

"I perfectly understand the ground rules," said Katzenberg. He recognized that Steven would always want to be home as early as possible to be with his family.

"All important things get done in my life," said Steven. "I'm still home most nights by six and I'm still home on weekends."

In 1996 Kate gave birth to a daughter, Destry, and she and Steven adopted a baby girl, Mikaela. All seven of Steven's children love DreamWorks cartoons, such as *Tiny Toon Adventures* and *Animaniacs,* as well as the company's video games. "That makes my kids really proud of me," Steven said. "They care volumes that my name precedes *Tiny Toons* and *Animaniacs*."

Would DreamWorks succeed? People wondered. Starting a new movie company was a risky business. Many had tried and failed. Some of the company's early films, such as *Amistad*, an antislavery story based on a historical event and directed by Steven, received good reviews but did poorly at the box office.

Then, in 1998, Amblin/DreamWorks SKG produced *Saving Private Ryan*, the most financially successful war movie to date. Steven directed the film and was

one of the producers. *Saving Private Ryan*, a World War II drama, tells of an eight-man mission that goes behind enemy lines to rescue a stranded paratrooper whose three older brothers have been killed in action. Their mother, at home in Iowa, has received the news of her loss all in one day. When the top general in Washington, D.C., hears about it, he feels compassionate and decides to send soldiers to find the sole surviving brother, Private Ryan, and bring him home.

"Where's the sense of risking the lives of the eight of us to save one guy?" says Private Reiben, one of the soldiers in the film, as they push deeper into enemy territory.

Their leader, Captain John Miller, played by Tom Hanks, responds, "We're talking about our duty as soldiers. We all have orders and we have to follow them."

"Miller has a very decent center," said Spielberg. "I think some of the most decent gestures, and some of the most humane moments in our history, happen during the most inhumane times of combat.

"I've kind of had an obsession with World War II that originated with my father, who fought in World War II in Burma," said Steven. "I think my dad planted the seeds when he told me war stories, stories that made me want to know more about it."

Steven had made his first war movies, *Fighter Squad* and *Escape to Nowhere*, when he was just a teenager. Now he wanted to tackle the subject again— but *not* as a typical Hollywood extravaganza. "The last thing we wanted to do in this picture," he said, "was use the war simply as a springboard for action-adventure. I was looking for realism all the time."

Steven began by meeting with D-Day veterans who had actually landed on Omaha Beach on June 6,

Steven with Tom Hanks, *opposite page.*

1944, one of the opening scenes of the movie. "I basically did a lot of research about D-Day," he said. The original script described the landing in five or six pages. Steven extended it to a twenty-five-minute sequence.

"I was trying to put chaos up on the screen," he said. "I wanted the audience, I wanted everybody, to feel the same as those green recruits that were just off those Higgins boats and had never seen combat before. Ninety-five percent of them hadn't. It was complete chaos."

Omaha Beach, on the coast of Normandy, France, is

"I was trying to put chaos up on the screen."

---

a protected historical landmark. "Omaha Beach is a place to visit and say prayers, not a place to re-create an event," said Steven. So his production designer looked for another location and found a remarkably similar beach in Ireland.

Before production started in August 1997, Steven hired Captain Dale Dye of the United States Marine Corps to put the actors through ten days of basic training in the field. Steven wanted the actors to understand that "we weren't playing around. We were making a serious picture about war."

Captain Dye said, "I immersed those actors in that lifestyle. If I've done my job right, at least they have an inkling of the deprivations, the hardships."

"It was the worst experience of my life," admits actor Edward Burns, who portrayed Private Reiben.

Tom Hanks went through the same ordeal as the other actors even though he is a two-time Academy

Award winner and one of Steven's best friends. "We hiked all over the place and it was raining and cold," said Hanks. "We did physical training at five o'clock in the morning. We slept on the ground and we ate food that came out of cans and were heated up on little tiny stoves and we had Dye yelling at us because we were doing things wrong."

Hanks recalls that Dye said to the men, "Look, you guys, you're not just being a bunch of actors

Steven on location with Tom Sizemore (left) and Tom Hanks (right), *above*. D-Day scene: Soldiers in Higgins boats landing on the beach, *opposite page*.

who are going to lollygag their way through a little war movie. You're embodying the souls of the fallen comrades who made the world safe for democracy. So you're not going to do that lightly. You're going to know the weaponry, you're going to know the tactics, you're going to know the background, you're going to know the history."

"After a day or two there was almost a revolt," says Marvin Levy. "'Do we really need to do this?' said the actors. 'I'll get a part in another movie.'"

Tom Hanks took on his own role as leader and rounded them up. "'We're making a movie,' said

"It's important to remember that these were people willing to die for their country."

Hanks. 'We've got to do this. All the men in that squad were here.'"

"After his talk," says Levy, "they followed him."

By the end of the basic training, the actors felt more like real soldiers. "It brought us closer together," says Tom Sizemore, who played Sergeant Horvath, known simply as Sarge. Author-historian Stephen Ambrose, a consultant on the project, said, "Men in combat develop something beyond friendship: They're ready to die for each other. That is caught just right in *Saving Private Ryan*."

It took about four weeks to shoot the reenactment of the massive landing on D-Day. Janus Kaminski, cinematographer of *Schindler's List*, was director of photography once again. Kaminski and Steven wanted the film to look like newsreel footage, so they used hand-held cameras for most of the film

Baby Steven with his father.

and toned down the color. They were inspired by black-and-white photos of the landing taken by Robert Capa for *Life* magazine. Steven did no storyboarding for this movie. "In that way," he said, "I was able to hit the sets much like a newsreel cameraman following soldiers into war."

The Irish army provided 750 extras for the D-Day scene. (Many of them had also performed in Mel Gibson's *Braveheart*.) The men were fed, clothed, and made up in fifteen groups of fifty. There weren't enough uniforms from World War II available, so the

The actors with Captain Dale Dye (center, with arms folded), in boot camp.

Tom Hanks in boot camp.

costume designer had to have three thousand authentic costumes made. The company that produced the original boots for the American troops constructed two thousand pairs for the movie using the same pattern. Then all the costumes and boots were put through an aging process to make them look battle-worn.

Steven wanted to present "the first truth about what battle is: silent death." Therefore, composer John Williams scored *no* music for the battle scenes and a minimum elsewhere in the film.

In his attention to authentic detail, Steven asked his father, "What were the cuss words used during the war?" His father answered, "FUBAR—Fouled Up Beyond All Recognition." That phrase—along with other remembered moments—became part of the script. Steven's father saw it at the premiere in Los Angeles and said, "I was completely blown away by the first twenty-five minutes of the invasion."

The movie opened on July 24, 1998. World War II veterans wept when they saw *Saving Private Ryan*. "This movie is about the veterans, it's *for* the veterans of World War II," said Steven. "It's important to remember that these were people willing to die for their country."

Critics hailed the movie as a masterpiece. At the 1999 Academy Awards, *Saving Private Ryan* won five Oscars, including a second one for Steven as Best Director.

"It was a gift to my dad, for sure. For, in the first place, doing what he did along with millions and millions of others to save Western civilization. He made his contribution, he was part of the war effort," said Steven.

"I also thanked him for being my dad and letting me make my movies and giving me five hundred dollars to make *Firelight* and backing my career, and not forcing me to go into electronics."

Coming Attractions

"I dream for a living," Steven said in a interview. "Once a month the sky falls on my head, I come to, and I see another movie I want to make. My problem is that my imagination won't turn off."

He continues to make movies that are entertainment as well as social statements. *A.I. (Artificial Intelligence)*, released in the summer of 2001, is a science-fiction film based on a short story by Brian Aldiss. The late Stanley Kubrick planned to produce it as a movie but wanted Steven to take over. A renowned filmmaker, Kubrick was Steven's friend as well as his idol.

The story tells of an eleven-year-old boy. "He is 4 feet, 6 inches tall," reads the movie poster. "He has brown hair. His love is real. But he is not." Twelve-year-old Haley Joel Osment, who was nominated for an Academy Award for his role in *Sixth Sense*, plays the boy. The movie features a score by John Williams and photography by Janus Kaminski. Steven himself wrote

"I dream for a living."

the script—the only script he's written since *Close Encounters*—and he directed the film.

In the movie *A.I.*, Steven fully explores themes that have intrigued him throughout his career. Childhood. Family. The need for love. As in *E.T.* and

Steven and Haley Joel Osment studying the script of *A.I.*

Empire of the Sun, his hero is a boy. This time, however, the boy is a robot named David. David has been manufactured as the perfect child. His assignment is to comfort grieving parents Monica and Henry. Their real son lies cryogenically frozen until a cure can be found for his terminal illness. But David longs to gain the love of his adoptive mother.

Like Pinocchio, one of Steven's favorite characters, the robot David wants desperately to become a real boy. He even searches for the Blue Fairy who has the power to transform him. "The story is told so well," wrote critic Andrew Sarris, "that it ends up being an overwhelmingly haunting experience as well as an exquisite work of art."

Five of Steven's films—*Schindler's List*, *E.T. The Extra-Terrestrial*, *Jaws*, *Raiders of the Lost Ark*, and *Close Encounters of the Third Kind*—have been included on the American Film Institute's list of the one hundred best movies of all time.

Steven Spielberg is still crazy for movies—watching them and creating them. He sees more than a hundred new films a year, and also some of his old favorites—*It's a Wonderful Life*, *Lawrence of Arabia*, and *The Godfather*. Although he has his own screening rooms at home and at Amblin, he enjoys going to movies at the theater. Steven has been spotted at the East Hampton Cinema on Long Island, buying popcorn for his family while they sit inside watching the previews.

When asked what projects he would like to do in the future, he said, "I haven't made a love story yet. A real love story. Oddly, I'd like to make an old-fashioned musical. Sing and talk, talk and sing. And dancing."

Or he might make a movie about himself and his family. His sister Anne has already written the script. It's called *I'll Be Home*, and is about a brother and sister who as adults go back to visit their childhood home. Steven has been considering doing it for years. "My big fear," he said, "is that my mom and dad won't like it and will think it's an insult and won't share my loving yet critical point of view about what it was like to grow up with them."

Steven's parents continue to exert a great influence on his work as he draws from his childhood memories in his films.

"It's a physical pleasure being on a set, making a movie—taking images out of your imagination and making them three-dimensional and solid," says Steven.

"It's magic."

Steven with Sue and Anne, *left*. Steven with (clockwise from right) Anne, Sue, and Nancy, *below*.

References and Resources

Books About Steven Spielberg

*Books suitable for younger readers

Baxter, John. *Steven Spielberg*. New York: HarperCollins Publishers, 1996.

*Collins, Tom. *Steven Spielberg: Creator of E.T.* Minneapolis: Dillon Press, 1983.

*Connolly, Sean. *Steven Spielberg: An Unauthorized Biography*. Des Plaines: Heinemann Library, 1999.

*Crawley, Tony. *The Steven Spielberg Story*. New York: Quill, 1983.

*Ferber, Elizabeth. *Steven Spielberg*. Philadelphia: Chelsea House Publishers, 2000.

Friedman, Lester D. and Brent Notbohm. *Steven Spielberg Interviews*. Jackson: University Press of Mississippi, 2000.

*Gish, Melissa. *Steven Spielberg*. Mankato, Wisconsin: Creative Education, 2000.

*Hargrove, Jim. *Steven Spielberg: Amazing Filmmaker*. Chicago: Children's Press, 1988.

*Mabery, D.L. *Steven Spielberg*. Minneapolis: Lerner Publications Company, 1986.

*Meachum, Virginia. *Steven Spielberg: Hollywood Filmmaker*. Springfield, New Jersey: Enslow Publishers, Inc., 1996.

McBride, Joseph. *Steven Spielberg: A Biography*. New York: DeCapo Press, 1999.

Palowski, Franciszek. *The Making of* Schindler's List. Secaucus, New Jersey: Carol Publishing Group, 1997.

Perry, George. *Steven Spielberg Close Up*. New York: Thunder's Mouth Press, 1998.

*Powers, Tom. *Steven Spielberg: Master Storyteller*. Minneapolis: Lerner Publications Company, 1997.

*Sanello, Frank. *Spielberg: The Man, The Movies, The Mythology*. Dallas: Taylor Publishing Company, 1996.

*Sinyard, Neil. *The Films of Steven Spielberg*. London: Bison Books Ltd., 1986.

Books About Movies

Katz, Ephraim. *The Film Encyclopedia*. New York: HarperCollins, 1998.

Lumet, Sidney. *Making Movies*. New York: Vintage Books, 1996.

Taub, Eric. *Gaffers, Grips, and Best Boys*. New York: St. Martin's Press, 1994.

Articles About Steven Spielberg

Benning, Jim. "Survivors of the Shoah." *Silicon Alley Reporter,* issue 27.

Corliss, Richard. "I Dream for a Living." *Time,* July 15, 1985.

——————. "Hey, Let's Put On a Show!" *Time,* March 27, 1995.

Gaydos, Steven. "Future the focus of Spielberg's passion." *Variety,* October 30–November 5, 2000.

Gumbel, Peter. "Making History." *The Wall Street Journal,* March 22, 1999.

Kenney, Linda Chion. "Spielberg promotes tolerance before rapt AASA audience." *The Conference Daily,* March 5, 2000.

Rahner, Mark. "Spielberg: Don't let Holocaust memories die." *The Seattle Times,* May 9, 2000.

Sheinkopf, Evelyn. "Archive's mission: tolerance education." *Variety,* October 30–November 5, 2000.

Spielberg, Steven. "The Autobiography of Peter Pan." *Time,* July 15, 1985.

"Steven Spielberg's Norman Rockwell." *Berkshire,* summer 1993.

"Teenage Cecil B." *Arizona Days and Ways magazine,* December 8, 1963.

Tugend, Tom. "Preservation Efforts." *Jewish Journal,* December 3, 1999.

Other Resources

Survivors of the Shoah Visual History Foundation. For more information, call toll-free 1-818-777-4673, or visit the foundation's website at www.shoahfoundation.org. You may also write to Shoah Foundation. P.O. Box 3168, Los Angeles, CA 90078-3168.

The Backyard National Children's Film Festival holds an annual contest for movies made by young people 18 and under. The finalists' entries are screened at a major Hollywood studio. For more information, visit www.backyardfilm.org. Lego, the manufacturer of the Lego & Steven Spielberg MovieMaker Set, is a sponsor of the contest.

Video and Audio Recordings

"Steven Spielberg." A&E Biography, March 17, 1999, and March 18, 1999. "Inside the Actors Studio." Show #506, Steven Spielberg. February 17, 1999.

Tom Hanks/Steven Spielberg, press conference for *Saving Private Ryan,* recording loaned by Daniel Neman, staff writer, *Richmond Times-Dispatch.*

Select Filmography (films used as reference for this book)

Films written and directed by Steven Spielberg

Fighter Squad, 1960.

Firelight, 1964.

Close Encounters of the Third Kind, 1977.

Films written and produced by Steven Spielberg

Poltergeist, 1982. (credit shared)

Films directed by Steven Spielberg

The Sugarland Express, 1974.

Jaws, 1975.

Raiders of the Lost Ark, 1981.

E.T. The Extra-Terrestrial, 1982.

Indiana Jones and the Temple of Doom, 1984.

The Color Purple, 1985.

Empire of the Sun, 1987.

Jurassic Park, 1993.

Schindler's List, 1993.

The Lost World: Jurassic Park, 1997.

Amistad, 1997.

Saving Private Ryan, 1998.

CD-ROM

Survivors: Testimonies of the Holocaust. Steven Spielberg and Survivors of the Shoah Visual History Foundation, 1998.

Sound Recordings

Williams, John. *Schindler's List.* Universal City Studios, Inc. and Amblin Entertainment, 1993

————. *E.T. The Extra-Terrestrial.* Universal CityStudios, 1992.

————. *Jaws.* Universal Pictures, 1975.

————. *John Williams' Greatest Hits 1969-1999.* Sony Music Entertainment, 1999.

Interviews by the Author

1. Leah Adler. April 12, 2000, May 3, 2000, and November 30, 2000, in person.
2. Arnold Spielberg, June 26, 2000, in person.
3. Anne Spielberg, August 17, 2000, and January 4, 2001, in person.
4. Sue Spielberg, April 25, 2000, telephone interview, and April 29, 2000, in person.
5. Anne, Sue, and Nancy Spielberg, June 24, 2000, in person.
6. John Williams, October 25, 2000, telephone interview.
7. Daisy Miller, May 10, 2000, in person.
8. Allen Daviau, August 30, 2000, in person.
9. Richard Dreyfuss, September 7, 2000, telephone interview.
10. Jerry Molen, September 7, 2000, phone interview.
11. Ariana Richards, November 29, 2000, in person.
12. Marvin Levy, December 7, 2000, and January 16, 2001, in person.

Glossary of Filmmaking Terms

Angle The camera's point of view that determines what the audience will see.

Close-up A shot taken from a short distance that shows an enlarged detail of a person or object.

Crane A large wheeled support that carries a camera on an arm that pivots, raises, and lowers.

Dailies Roughly assembled prints of scenes shot the previous day, shown in the order they were filmed.

Documentary A factual film depicting actual events with real people and places.

Dolly A wheeled platform on which a camera is mounted so that it can follow the actors by moving through the set.

Editing The process of selecting and assembling motion picture shots in a sequence.

Extras Members of the cast who speak no lines and appear as part of the background.

Film sizes Movie film comes in different widths: 16mm is generally used for student films and documentaries; 35mm is the industry standard for theatrical motion pictures and high-end television movies.

Fixed-focus camera An amateur camera with a lens that films objects best from a distance of six feet or more.

Handheld camera A portable motion-picture camera that the cameraman holds in his hands and steadies against his body, without a tripod.

Location Any place away from the studio selected for shooting.

Matching shots To make scenes shot in different light at different times of day look the same.

Producer The person responsible for the movie from start to finish. He or she chooses the project, hires the screenwriter, plans the budget and shooting schedule, may or may not direct the picture, supervises postproduction, and finally coordinates distribution and release.

Production Shooting the film.

Postproduction Editing and preparing the film for distribution.

Preproduction Planning the film: choosing locations, designing the set, and hiring cast and crew.

Production designer Also called the art director. The production designer plans how the film should look, often working with the costume designer and cinematographer.

Rushes Prints of scenes shot the previous day that are hurriedly printed overnight.

Script supervisor Follows the production report, listing what has been accomplished during a day's shooting, and reports to the assistant director.

Serials Films with many episodes (usually action-adventure) that are presented one installment at a time, each ending with a cliffhanger.

Shorts Films that run thirty minutes or less, such as cartoons, newsreels, and comedies. Shorts were sometimes added to a movie program until the mid-1940s.

Soundstage A soundproof studio equipped for the production of films with sound.

Soundtrack A narrow band on the left side of sound film which carries recorded patterns of dialogue, music, and sound effects.

Storyboard A layout of sketches in sequence that outline the main action of a film.

Tight shot A shot in which the subject fills most of the frame.

Wide shot The master shot that includes everything that will appear in the scene and is usually filmed first.

Zoom lens A type of lens that enables the cameraman to move quickly from a long shot to a close-up of the same subject without having to adjust the focus.

Photo Credits

Courtesy of the Steven Spielberg Archives: opposite title page, and pages 4 (bottom), 5, 8, 9 (bottom), 14 (bottom), 18, 20 (top), 27, 32, 48, 58 (bottom), 84 (top)

Courtesy of Anne Spielberg: pages 4 (top), 9 (top), 11 (top and center), 14 (top), 15, 26, 34, 56 (bottom), 58 (top), 87 (bottom), 94

Courtesy of Anne Spielberg and the Steven Spielberg Archives: pages 11 (bottom) and 14 (bottom)

Courtesy of Sue Spielberg: pages 6, 10 (top and center), 12, 16 (top and bottom), 20 (bottom), 22 (top and bottom), 36, 73 (right), 87 (top)

Courtesy of Sue and Anne Spielberg: page 13

Courtesy of the Steven Spielberg Archives and *Arizona Days and Ways* magazine, December 1963, Photo by Ralph Camping: page 7

Copyright © 2001 by Universal City Studios, Inc. Courtesy of Universal Studios Publishing Rights, a division of Universal Studios Licensing, Inc. All rights reserved: pages 10 (bottom), 24, 25, 29, 31, 33, 37, 38, 40, 41, 74 (photo by Peter Iovino)

Copyright © 2001 by Universal City Studios, Inc. Courtesy of Universal Studios Publishing Rights, a division of Universal Studios Licensing, Inc. All rights reserved. Copyright © 2001 by Amblin Entertainment: pages 23, 49, 50, 51, 60 and 61 (photos by Murray Close), 62, 63, 64, 65

Courtesy of Amblin Entertainment: page 55

Photograph by Bonnie Schiffman: page 17

Credit: "Close Encounters of the Third Kind" © 1977 Columbia Pictures Industries, Inc. All Rights Reserved. Courtesy of Columbia Pictures: pages 43 and 44.

Copyright © Disney Enterprises, Inc.: page 45

Kobal Collection: page 46

Courtesy of Lucasfilm Ltd. Credit: "Raiders of the Lost Ark," © 1981 Lucasfilm Ltd. and ™. All Rights Reserved. Used under authorization. Unauthorized duplication is a violation of applicable law: page 47

"The Color Purple © 1985 Warner Bros. Inc. All Rights Reserved": page 56 (top)

"Empire of the Sun © 1987 Warner Bros. Inc. All Rights Reserved": page 59 (top)

Collection of the Norman Rockwell Museum, Norman Rockwell Art Collection Trust. Printed by permission of the Norman Rockwell Family Trust, Copyright © 1943 the Norman Rockwell Family Trust: page 59 (bottom left)

Courtesy of Ariana Richards: page 66

Courtesy of Jerry Molen: page 69 (left)

Courtesy of the Survivors of the Shoah Visual History Foundation: pages 75, 76, 77

Photo credit: David James. Copyright © 1993 by Universal City Studios, Inc. Courtesy of Universal Studios Publishing Rights, a division of Universal Studios Licensing, Inc. All Rights Reserved. Copyright © 2001 Amblin Entertainment: pages 67, 68, 69 (right), 70, 71, 72, 73 (left).

Photo by David James for the motion picture *Saving Private Ryan* © 1998 DreamWorks, L.L.C., and Paramount Pictures, reprinted with permission by DreamWorks, L.L.C.: pages 79, 83 (top)

Photo by David James. Courtesy of DreamWorks, L.L.C., and Paramount Pictures Corporation and Amblin Entertainment: pages 80, 82, 83 (bottom), 84 (bottom)

Photo by David James. Copyright © 2001 Warner Bros. Pictures and DreamWorks, L.L.C.: page 86

Photo by Joan Yarfitz: page 25

Cover credits:

Front: *E.T.* (top and bottom center; also spine photo), *Jaws* (bottom left), and *Jurassic Park* (bottom right), all courtesy of Universal Studios Publishing Rights, a division of Universal Studios Licensing, Inc., and courtesy of Amblin Entertainment, Inc. *Jurassic Park* photo by Murray Close. Second from left, bottom: Photo by David James, courtesy of Universal Studios Publishing Rights, a division of Universal Studios Licensing, Inc., and courtesy of Amblin Entertainment, Inc. Second from right, bottom: Courtesy of the Steven Spielberg Archives.

Back: Left and right, Courtesy of the Steven Spielberg Archives. Second from left and center: Courtesy of Anne Spielberg. Second from right: Courtesy of Sue Spielberg.

All photos copyright © 2001.

Index

Page numbers in italics indicate picture captions.

Adler, Bernie, 22, 73, *73*, 74
Adler, Leah (mother), *4*, 6, 8, 9, *9,*
    10, 11, 12, *12,* 15, *16,* 17–18,
    19, *20,* 21, 22, *22,* 25, 28, *36,*
    53, 68, 73, *73,* 74, 86
A. I. (Artificial Intelligence), 85
Aldiss, Brian, 85
Allen, Karen, 48
Allen, Woody, 45
Amblin', 26–27, *26,* 52
Amblin Entertainment, 54–55
Ambrose, Stephen, 82
American Tail, An, 10, *10*
Amistad, 79
Atherton, William, *32*
Attenborough, Richard, 53, 63, *65*

Bale, Christian, 57
Ballard, J. G., 57, 58
Barrymore, Drew, 51, *51,* 52
Barwood, Hal, 32
Benchley, Peter, 36
Bill, Tony, 25
Brown, David, 36
Burns, Edward, 81
Burris, Ralph, 24, 25

Canby, Vincent, 53
Capshaw, Kate, 54, 58, *58,* 73, 79
Cassavetes, John, 25

Close Encounters of the Third Kind,
    8, 14, 42–45, 46, 51, 52, 85
Color Purple, The, 57
Color Purple, The (Walker), 55–57
Commando Cody, 46, *46*
Coppola, Francis Ford, 25, 32
Crawford, Joan, 28–30, *28*
Crichton, Michael, 60, 63

Daviau, Allen, 25–26, *25,* 52, 57,
    58
De Palma, Brian, 39
Diana, Princess, 66, *66*
DiCaprio, Leonardo, 77
DreamWorks SKG, 78, 79
Dreyfuss, Richard, 36–39, *36,* 40,
    41, *41,* 42, 44
Duel, 30–32, *30,* 34
Dye, Dale, 81, 82, *84*

Empire of the Sun, 57–58, *58*
Escape to Nowhere, 18, 20, 81
E.T. The Extra-Terrestrial, 14, 19,
    22, *22, 48,* 51–53, *51,* 54, 55,
    67, 85

Fields, Verna, 40
Fighter Squad, 17, 81
Firelight, 4–8, *8,* 19, 20, 44, 84
Ford, Harrison, *46,* 48
Freedom from Fear (Rockwell), 58,
    58

Geffen, David, 78
Gilmore, Bill, 34
Goldberg, Whoopi, 57

Gottlieb, Carl, 36, 39
Guffrey, Cary, 42

Haginere, Serge, 25
Hanks, Tom, 81–82, *81, 82*
Hawn, Goldie, 32–34, *32,* 35

I'll Be Home, 86
Indiana Jones and the Temple of
    Doom, 54, 58
Irving, Amy, 45, 48, 54, 57, 58

Jaws, 36–41, *36,* 42, 45, 55, 85
Jaws (Benchley), 36
Jiminy Cricket, 44, *45*
Jones, Quincy, 55
Jurassic Park, 60–66, *60, 63*
Jurassic Park (Crichton), 60

Kael, Pauline, 35
Kaminsky, Janus, 69, 74, 82, 85
Katzenberg, Jeffrey, 78, 79
Keneally, Thomas, 67
Kennedy, Kathleen, 53, 54, 55, 65
King, Stephen, 30
Koepp, David, 66
Kubrick, Stanley, 85

Lanzmann, Claude, 69
Last Days, The, 77
Last Gunfight, The (*The Last Gun;*
    The Last Shootout), 16
Last Train Wreck, The, 15
Lean, David, 32
Levy, Marvin, 70, 78, 82
Lost World: Jurassic Park, The, 66

Lucas, George, 32, 46, 48, 54, 65
Lustig, Branko, 69–70, *69, 76*

MacNaughton, Robert, 51
Marshall, Frank, 55
Matheson, Richard, 30
Mathison, Melissa, 48, 51
Mattey, Bob, 39
Mazzello, Joseph, 63
Mermelstein, Mel, 76
Miller, Daisy, 76
Molen, Jerry, 69, *69,* 70, 74, 76
Murren, Dennis, 65

Neeson, Liam, 69–70, *70*
Night Gallery, 28–30
Nitzan, Adi, 70

Osment, Haley Joel, 85, *85*

Page, Leopold, 67, 68, *68, 70*
Perlman, Itzhak, 74
Poltergeist, 10, 12, 14
Posner, Bernard (uncle), *12*
Posner, Jennie (grandmother), 9,
    10, 11, *12*
Posner, Philip (grandfather), 10,
    10, 12

Raiders of the Lost Ark, 46–48, *46,*
    51, 54, 85
Rambaldi, Carlo, 52
Reagan, Nancy, 53
Reagan, Ronald, 53
Rich, Frank, 45
Richards, Ariana, 63, 65, 66, *66*

Robbins, Matthew, 32
Rockwell, Norman, 55, 58, *58*
Ryder, Winona, 77

Saving Private Ryan, 17, 79–84, *79*
Scheider, Roy, 40, *41*
Schindler, Oskar, 67
Schindler's List, 10, 66, 67–74, 75,
    85
Schindler's List (Keneally), 67
Serling, Rod, 28
Sheinberg, Sidney J., 27, *27*
Shoah, 69
Shoah Foundation, 75–77, 79
Silvers, Chuck, 20–21, 22, 24, 27
Sizemore, Tom, 82, *82*
Slipstream, 25–26, 52
Smith, Cecil, 32
Sollenberger, Jim, 17
Spielberg, Anne (sister), 6, 7,
    11–12, *11, 12,* 14, *14,* 15, 16,
    18, 22, 26, *26,* 35, *36,* 41, 55,
    57, 68, 74, 75, 86, *86*
Spielberg, Arnold (father), 4, *4,*
    7–8, 9, *9, 12,* 14, 16, 17, 18,
    19, 21, 22, 24–25, 28, 40, 77,
    81, 84, *84,* 86
Spielberg, Becky (grandmother),
    73, *73*
Spielberg, Destry (daughter), 79
Spielberg, Jessica (daughter), 58,
    73
Spielberg, Leah (mother), *see*
    Adler, Leah
Spielberg, Max Samuel (son), 57,
    73

Spielberg, Mikaela (daughter), 79
Spielberg, Nancy (sister), 7, *7,* 11,
    12, *12,* 16, 18, *20,* 21, *22,* 44,
    45, 74, *86*
Spielberg, Sasha (daughter), 58,
    73
Spielberg, Sawyer (son), 73
Spielberg, Sue (sister), 6, *7,* 11,
    11, 12, *12,* 14, *14, 16,* 18, *20,*
    21, 22, *22,* 35, *36,* 41, 44, 45,
    57, 86
Spielberg, Theo (son), 58, 73
Star Wars, 45, 46
Stoppard, Tom, 58
Strauss, Bert, *75*
Sugarland Express, The, 32–35, *32*
Survivors of the Shoah Visual
    History Foundation, 75–77

This Is a Dog's Life, 21–22
Thomas, Henry, *22,* 51, *51,* 52

Walker, Alice, 55–57
Wallace, Dee, 52
Weaver, Dennis, *30,* 32
Will, George F., 53
Williams, John, 35, 40, 44, 53,
    73–74, 84, 85
Winfrey, Oprah, 57
Winston, Stan, *64,* 65, *65*

Zanuck, Richard, 36, 39
Zsigmond, Vilmos, 34